UNCERTAINTY

Printed and bound in the United States.

Uncertainty is *Boston Review* Forum 20 (46.4)

Caley Horan's essay is adapted with permission from Insurance Era: Risk, Governance, and the Privatization of Security in Postwar America *by Caley Horan, published by The University of Chicago Press. © 2021 by The University of Chicago. All rights reserved.*

To become a member, visit bostonreview.net/membership/

For questions about donations and major gifts, contact Dan Manchon, dan@bostonreview.net

For questions about memberships, call 877-406-2443 or email Customer_Service@bostonreview.info.

Boston Review
PO Box 390568
Cambridge, MA 02139

ISSN: 0734-2306 / ISBN: 978-1-946511-66-9

CONTENTS

ESSAYS

What Good Can Dreaming Do?

We Don't Know, But Let's Try It

Contributors

EDITORS' NOTE

Joshua Cohen & Deborah Chasman

NEARLY TWO YEARS into a global pandemic, uncertainty has profoundly unsettled both our personal and political lives. Some of its sources are epistemic: When should schools reopen for in-person learning? How long will vaccine immunity last? Do rising prices threaten economic recovery? Others are sharply existential: How will I pay rent next month? Can I travel safely? Will I see my loved one again? At perhaps no other moment in the twenty-first century has there been such widespread unease about what the future holds.

What does this crisis of certainty mean for society? As enduring debates over pandemic policy have made clear, uncertainty is particularly consequential where it intersects with political power. Leading this issue's forum, Sheila Jasanoff, pioneering scholar of science and technology studies, argues that public policy could benefit from a much more serious acknowledgment of uncertainty. Her essay begins with the striking failures of the U.S. pandemic response, despite decades of warning from public health experts that such a crisis was inevitable. The problem, Jasanoff contends, "was to overestimate the certainty of our predictions and our capacity for control." In place of the hubris of technocratic expertise, Jasanoff calls for "technologies of humility"—institutional mechanisms, including greater citizen participation, for incorporating a wider range of experience and views in our schemes of democratic governance. Respondents to Jasanoff consider other causes of pandemic mismanagement and ask whether humility is the best response.

Other contributors extend the discussion of uncertainty beyond COVID-19. Uncertainty not only shapes what we do, Oded Na'aman notes, but also how we feel, and philosophy offers a fount of wisdom when we imagine the worst. Nor is uncertainty necessarily paralyzing. As Simon Torracinta observes, the late social scientist Albert O. Hirschman saw it as an opportunity. Perfect planning is impossible, he thought, but that shouldn't stop us from trying to build a more just world and learning from our collective experience. In the face of the immense challenges before us—and uncertainty about how best to solve them—we could do far worse than share his "bias for hope."

HUMILITY IN PANDEMIC TIMES

Sheila Jasanoff

THE COVID-19 PANDEMIC has confounded the world's expectations at every turn. It began in surprise, continued with chaos, and devolved into conspiracy theories. From a policy standpoint, it gave the lie to our prepandemic imaginations of order and control. Public health experts, after all, had warned of an outbreak for decades. But despite its prominence among the grand global challenges that successive U.S. presidents were advised to take seriously, it still caught this nation and many others flatfooted. Nineteen months into the pandemic and counting, the balance sheet of losses and gains in the United States leans negative across public health, the economy, and democratic politics. How can we begin to make sense of a widely predicted crisis that, by late October 2021, had carried off nearly 5 million lives worldwide, stalled economies, and placed unprecedented strains on social ties and personal liberty?

The mistake, I argue, was to overestimate the certainty of our predictions and our capacity for control. Prediction as a policy tool focuses on identifying chains of causation and assessing their likelihood before bad things happen. That approach has scored great successes, most notably in alerting the world to the threat of climate change well before droughts, wildfires, and record-breaking storms showed ordinary people that weather was turning calamitous. Prediction, however, also falters under the weight of its own ambitions. Disasters happen, and hindsight often reveals overconfidence in the pictures of nature and society on which predictions were based. The makers of thalidomide and diethylstilbestrol did not test for side effects on children born to pregnant women. NASA launched the Challenger without fully analyzing data on the performance of the rocket's O-ring seals at unusually cold temperatures. Promoters of biofuels failed to calculate the effects of incentivizing these crops on the production of essential food grains. The Fukushima Daiichi planners did not count on a 9.0-magnitude earthquake or a fifteen-meter tsunami at the site of the nuclear power plant.

To counter prediction's problems of complexity, ignorance, and uncertainty, the policy world recommends precaution. Commonly traced to German environmental policy of the early 1970s, the precautionary principle—or *Vorsorgeprinzip*—instructs public authorities to plan ahead and act to prevent serious harm to humans and the environment even in the absence of full scientific certainty. This principle has been widely adopted in international agreements such as the 1992 Rio Declaration on Environment and Development and the European Union's Maastricht Treaty of the same year. Yet precaution remains deeply controversial. Critics frequently dismiss it as a recipe for inaction and stagnation. A notable U.S. example is Cass Sunstein's scathing denunciation of Europe's reliance on precaution as fear-driven, paralyzing, and self-blinding.

Advocates of precaution insist that the principle does not stand for passivity or resignation. It was developed precisely to enable and justify prudent forward movement to serve the common good, even when the consequences of acting cannot be completely known. Still, an asymmetry remains that works in favor of prediction and discourages precaution. It is easy to assert our calculative power and deploy our technologies, but less easy to say when to hold back or how not to act. Can one operationalize the precautionary mindset as a positive alternative to the known failures of prediction?

What I offer here is a plea for humility, not merely as a stance of modesty vis-à-vis the powerful and still poorly understood forces of nature and society, but also as a practice of reasoning and policy that accepts uncertainty as its foundation and harm mitigation as its goal. If we mean to do better against the inevitable next time, how should we diagnose what went wrong in the preparations the world had for so long been cultivating, and how should we plan more effectively for the next crisis that will surely come?

The answer cannot be simply to embrace a policy of preparedness toward every possible hazard. To be prepared is a stance of courage and conviction. It implies not merely that one is ready for all contingencies, but that one is confident of one's ability to meet and overcome them. Britain's Robert Baden-Powell, who founded the Boy Scouts and chose their motto "Be Prepared," explained that it meant one should be ready "for any old thing." The United States Coast Guard glosses its motto—*semper paratus* (always ready)—to mean that all of its resources are available to meet the nation's needs and to play "an integral role in mission execution." Preparedness, in short, is a heroic, can-do posture, bravely denying the possibility of defeat.

Humility, by contrast, admits that defeat is possible. It occupies the nebulous zone between preparedness and precaution by asking a moral question: not what we can achieve with what we have, but how we should act given that we cannot know the full consequences of our actions. Thought of in this way, humility addresses the questions perennially raised by critics of precaution and refutes the charges of passivity. Confronted on many fronts by riddles too knotty to solve, must society choose either to do nothing or to move aggressively forward as if risks don't matter and resources are limitless? Decades of effort to protect human health and the environment suggest that the choice is not so stark or binary. There is a middle way, the way of humility, that permits steps to be taken here and now in order to forestall worst-case scenarios later. It implements precaution by unheroic but also more ethical means, through what I call technologies of humility: institutional mechanisms—including greater citizen participation—for incorporating memory, experience, and concerns for justice into our schemes of governance and public policy. This is a proactive, historically informed, and analytically robust method that asks not just what we can do but who might get hurt, what happened when we tried before, whose perceptions were systematically ignored, and what protections are in place if we again guess wrong.

An Anatomy of Preparedness

SINCE 1945, when the Los Alamos physicists got their first taste of science as sin, the United States has been preparing for catastrophic events that place the nation's health, security, and identity at extreme risk. Indeed, the shock of catastrophe came even earlier, at Pearl Harbor in 1941, when the U.S. government failed to read the tea leaves of Japan's military ambitions in time to stave off a devastating attack on U.S. soil. Nor did the surprises stop with the war's end. Every major U.S. crisis since World War II—the Cuban Missile Crisis, defeat in Vietnam, Three Mile Island, 9/11, the Great Recession, COVID-19, and the rapid fall of Kabul to the Taliban—has generated the same dynamics of self-questioning. Why did we not know when the information was there to be known? Why were we caught unprepared?

The short answer is that we embraced preparedness when we should have opted for precaution. We invested mainly in the arts of control when instead we might have chosen the ethos of responsibility. The pandemic offers an especially illuminating case on which to hang this argument. In some sense this was the most expected of all unexpected events. To borrow UK prime minister Boris Johnson's poignant phrase about the sudden surrender of Afghanistan, COVID-19 was the "chronicle of an event foretold." Since the Great Spanish Flu of 1918–1920 took more lives than fighting did in World War I, we have known that deadly respiratory illness can spread around the world with great speed and ruinous impact. Variants from that century-old pandemic still plague the world in the form of seasonal influenza viruses that cause hundreds of thousands of deaths each year. Since then, rising populations, closer contact between people and virus-incubating animals such as birds and bats, and above all the growing mobility of human populations have amply set the stage for recurrent pandemics.

There were many early warnings before COVID-19. In 1994 science writer Laurie Garrett shocked the American reading public with her best-selling book *The Coming Plague*, which warned of rampant epidemics in a "world out of balance." Widely praised for its dense coverage of the epidemiology of past infectious disease outbreaks, Garrett's book gloomily concluded that in the long standoff between humans and microbes, "the microbes were winning." The years before and since offered many examples on scales that should have caused people to worry, and worry they did. AIDS appeared in 1981 and, though infections and deaths peaked in 1995, forty years of the disease claimed roughly as many U.S. lives as eighteen months of COVID-19. Other viral disease epidemics with transnational spread occurred at frequent intervals: SARS-CoV-1 in 2003, MERS-CoV in 2012, and Ebola in 2014.

Even popular culture did its bit to raise awareness. In an example of life following art, former UK health secretary Matt Hancock told the BBC in February 2021 that the 2011 film *Contagion* had taught him the importance of having enough vaccine supply for the entire population and being clear about the order of priority. In fact, after badly fumbling the first phases of the pandemic, Britain was widely acclaimed for its vaccine rollout, "the front line in what has become the most ambitious peacetime mass mobilization in modern British history."

Public and private risk assessors strove for years to prepare responsibly for the great plague that all were sure would come. Possibly the most visible international effort, the Global Health Security Index (GHSI), came about in response to the Ebola epidemic as a joint project among three expert bodies with deep knowledge of risk: the Nuclear Threat Initiative, the Johns Hopkins Center for Health Security, and the Economist Intelligence Unit. The 2019 GHSI provided a preparedness snapshot for each of the 195 parties to the International Health Regulations. Billing itself as the most comprehensive benchmarking of nations' capacity to deal with infectious disease outbreaks, the GHSI organized its findings under 6 categories, 34 indicators, and 140 questions. Unsurprisingly perhaps, the United States and the United Kingdom scored highest while small, war-torn, and politically unstable states fared worst, with North Korea, Somalia, and Equatorial Guinea bringing up the rear in national capacity.

Meanwhile, public health experts in the United States and elsewhere mined historical outbreaks to construct game plans for future epidemics. The Obama administration left its successor a detailed Playbook for Early Response to High-Consequence Emerging Infectious Disease Threats and Biological Incidents. The document divided the risk world into two rubrics: one for an international response geared toward outbreaks anywhere in the world, with Ebola as its model, and the other for a domestic response to address disease outbreaks within the United States. A key recommendation was to create a "dashboard" signaling the severity of the threat, from green for normal operations to deep red once a threat was established. The playbook, like the GHSI, proposed categories and indicators to assess the risks involved, though its framework showed greater awareness that epidemics are social as well as biological events. For instance, the playbook flagged humanitarian impacts, political stability, and public concern as relevant dimensions of risk. It was a valiant attempt to identify all the relevant questions that should be asked at the onset of an outbreak, compiled with the earnest attention that one might expect in a first-rate "policy analysis exercise" at one of our top public policy schools.

A third document to set beside the GHSI and the playbook appeared early in the pandemic, on April 1, 2020. This was an editorial in the *New England Journal of Medicine* titled "Ten Weeks to Crush the Curve." The author, Harvey Fineberg, is one of the nation's foremost public health experts, former provost and dean of public health at Harvard, former president of what is now the National Academy of Medicine, and chair since March 2020 of the Standing Committee on Emerging Infectious Diseases and twenty-first-century Century Health Threats. With stringent public health measures already in place, Fineberg's editorial was not so much a guide to preparedness as a manifesto on how to respond when the walls against infection have already been breached. From its first sentence, the editorial adopted President Donald J. Trump's framing of the problem as a declaration of war. Fineberg's six-step program, pitched as a call to arms, aimed to bring the virus under control and set the economy back on track by June 6, 2020, the anniversary of D-Day. Step one was to "establish unified command."

All three documents—the GHSI, the playbook, and the Fineberg editorial—earn high marks as delineations of steps that intelligent and decisive policymakers should take in their efforts to be prepared for emerging infectious diseases. But how do these well-defined preparations hold up against a world in which the unexpected is the order of the day? In spite of their disparate origins and different purposes, two things can be said about these three efforts. It is clear in retrospect that none of the authors paid much attention to the swiftly moving, shape-shifting events, cutting across geopolitical lines, that impede rational analysis and effective response during an actual pandemic. This is partly because all emerged from a militaristic mindset, in which the goal was clear, public buy-in was presumed, and challenges were seen as more logistic than political—more a matter of mobilizing resources, as the Coast Guard pledges to do, than of exploring how to generate the will to act or the risks, costs, and distributive impact of wrong decisions.

The Unraveling

FAST FORWARD to October 2021. According to the Johns Hopkins Coronavirus Research Center, the United States, which led the GHSI as top scorer in preparedness, has the highest number of recorded COVID-19 deaths in the world, a staggering 740,000. The UK, ranked number two in the GHSI, has recorded more total deaths than any EU country. More tellingly, Britain ranks ahead of most major EU countries in deaths per 100,000 population. By contrast Germany, placed at 14 in the GHSI, ranks 22 in the number of deaths per million in the European Economic Area plus Britain, well below the UK in tenth place. Clearly, preparedness and performance were not perfectly aligned. As one influential team of observers concluded, there was an "extreme discrepancy between expected and actual performance for most countries."

And what of the playbook's impact on the U.S. response to COVID-19? None was detectable, and its very existence proved to be a point of controversy. In May 2020 Senator Mitch McConnell criticized the Obama administration for not leaving any guidance on a possible pandemic, falsely claiming that its experts had miscalculated the threat as a rare, once-in-a-century event. PBS reviewed the evidence and found McConnell's assertion blatantly untrue. Interestingly, however, the PBS assessment left open the question of the playbook's relevance: "whether the Obama plan was dated because it dealt with lessons learned from earlier outbreaks that may not apply to the current pandemic." Datedness, however, was not the playbook's most important problem: it was overconfidence in the nation's willingness to set aside politics and act in unison for the common good.

As to Fineberg's plan for all-out mobilization, June 6, 2020, came and went, and so did June 6, 2021. Instead of crushing the curve, in late summer of 2021 the United States entered a new phase of dangerously rising caseloads as the Delta variant created a map of intensified infection. The virus that should have been conquered a year back according to Fineberg's script was no longer quite the same virus. Nor had U.S. governance ever involved the centralized control that the nation's leading public health experts yearned for. Mask mandates crystallized the conflict and turmoil that still surround efforts to fight the novel coronavirus. The return of indoor masking even in well-vaccinated cities such as Boston spelled one kind of defeat. The microbes were gaining the upper hand again. In less excusable confrontations, the governors of Florida and Texas went to war against their own cities and school districts to prevent masking orders for students from taking effect—not exactly a picture of efficient, centralized high command in action. And the tarnish of breakthrough infections and vaccine hesitancy partly dimmed even the luster of savior vaccines developed, approved, and rolled out at breakneck speed.

A Diagnostic Moment

COVID-19'S DISASTROUS PROGRESS around the world brought to light something we had conveniently forgotten, or sidelined, over many decades of success in global efforts to understand and combat human disease: to a greater or lesser extent, securing public health and public safety requires human beings to give up aspects of their liberty in the interests of a common good. Building the regime of public health sovereignty is thus a profoundly political project, not simply a matter of technical knowledge and logistics. We may make those sacrifices willingly, in the name of science and communal benefit, but there are limits and it takes a special kind of work for governments to hold on to people's allegiance even in times of crisis.

To what extent did the advocates of preparedness take the politics of public health into account? All were aware of possible political constraints, but the specifics of that awareness took different forms, reflecting different appraisals of public health institutions' authority and expertise. At one pole we have Fineberg's call for total national wartime mobilization to crush the curve. To be sure, this was to be a democratic process. The fifth step in his six-point program was for the nation's leadership to "inspire and mobilize the public." But the actions Fineberg called for to inspire and mobilize presupposed United States that never was, or had long since ceased to be.

In particular, Fineberg imagined a United States in which a respected Postal Service would join with "willing private companies" to deliver hand sanitizer and surgical masks to every door. In reality, the early months of the epidemic saw everyone scrambling and hoarding to get access to such essentials as hand sanitizer and toilet paper, because supply chains failed and stores were entirely out of it. A colleague of mine won Zoom ovations from others at a faculty meeting because she had impressed her aged mother, teen-age children, and husband into making masks at home, a shining example of U.S. individualism rising to the challenge of the moment. At about the same time, I read enviously that the Japanese government, behaving more like Fineberg's unified command, was distributing two reusable cloth face masks to every household because drugstores and shops had run out of supplies. We got our own first masks not from any U.S. source but from a Chinese colleague who had obtained extras from overseas relatives.

In its comprehensive estimates of national capacities, the GHSI also acknowledges a central role for politics, so central evidently as to remain unexplored and unquestioned. The executive summary notes: "Knowing the risks, however, is not enough. Political will is needed to protect people from the consequences of epidemics, to take action to save lives, and to build a safer and more secure world." But *whose* political will, how activated, and how incorporated into the model? One may ask how a model of national capabilities built mainly on measurable indicators of health security was intended to account for such an intangible and volatile concept. Indeed, there is little evidence that the GHSI model incorporated variables such as federalism, political polarization and trust, income inequality, racial disparities, or marginalization of groups and regions in its calculations of preparedness. More foundationally, the GHSI assumed that all nations agree it is in their collective best interest to act in unison in a pandemic. Sadly, the chronicle of COVID-19—from the still unresolved question of how the virus first infected humans, to the surprising persistence of vaccine hesitancy—contradicts that basic assumption.

The playbook offers the most explicit statement of the political preconditions that would make its approach work. The domestic rubric, for instance, begins sensibly enough with the observation that, early in the trajectory of emergence, more will be unknown than known, and decisionmakers will have to act on incomplete information. Most of the succeeding assumptions, however, were based on ideals of ordered democracy dating from a less divisive time. They were quickly upended by unfolding events, positioning the United States as a "chaos country" in a comparative study I helped conduct during 2020. Notably, the U.S. government did not use all powers at its disposal to slow and mitigate the spread of disease, the National Security Council did not play the prescribed coordinating role, and states continued to wield a determining hand in policy, belying the expectation that the public would turn to the U.S. government for a concerted response.

It may be tempting to rejoin that human minds are fallible, and prediction and preparedness are at best guidelines for systematic analysis, not prescriptions for failsafe action. One might also argue that careful attention to the playbook's checklist approach might have prevented embarrassing slip-ups such as the French government being unaware in its early modeling exercises that there were direct flights between Paris and Wuhan, the pandemic's ground zero. But in fact the playbook and the Fineberg editorial have very much the look of blueprints, and the GHSI was less a map of the terrain than a guide to action: to "spur measurable changes in national health security and improve international capability" to address the "omnipresent risks" of a pandemic. Nor is the mismatch between expectation and performance limited to this pandemic alone. Our persistent failure to be prepared in times of crisis calls for another mindset, coupled to a deeper sensitivity toward the moral consequences of not knowing.

Technologies of Humility

PREPAREDNESS TODAY is chain-linked to the power of computing. With massive advances in data science and technology, humankind is in a position to process information about almost anything that moves on the planet at sweeping scales and speeds. Capability feeds ambition. From climate change to consumer choice, we have grown used to the power of prediction, thereby imputing a presumption of regularity and a capacity for control to every aspect of human affairs.

The shocks of our era should remind us that such Promethean dreams need to be curbed by the limits of prediction. To be sure, technologists of preparedness may object that such awareness is already built into their methods. Garbage in, garbage out, as the computer scientists put it: everyone knows that bad inputs produce flawed outputs, and predictions are only as good as the data they rest on. Yet, too often imperfection is imagined only as a matter of defective data and erroneous calculation. From this vantage point, the chief lesson of failure is to get more data, improve the models, and do the same thing, only better, next time. The ethics and politics of prediction pass unnoticed, though if we care about the consequences of our action or inaction, these are the dimensions that should concern us most.

A Schmidt Futures Forum on Preparedness convened in January 2021 offered striking examples of such epistemic narrowing. Fineberg offered a brief keynote in which he extolled the value of science for policy but noted the need for a "high level of humility" in the face of what is not known and the diversity of possible viewpoints. He then joined a panel of four distinguished international public servants who addressed the mistakes and failings of science and science advice during the first year of the pandemic. Former U.S. Navy undersecretary Richard Danzig introduced the panel by echoing Fineberg's appeal to humility and urged the guests to consider whether science had failed to account adequately for the vagaries of human behavior. In response, Margaret Hamburg, former FDA commissioner and a founder of the Nuclear Threat Initiative, revealed her continued allegiance to the preparedness paradigm, in which pandemics are primarily biological and actions fail mainly because science didn't try to know soon enough what we all know we should have known. Citing virus variants, immune responses, and asymptomatic carriage as primary examples, Hamburg spoke about "efforts to identify critical gaps in knowledge that would affect the contours and control measures for this pandemic."

In terms of the epistemic typology that Donald Rumsfeld made famous, Hamburg's emphasis was on known unknowns, the problems that science should have more aggressively pursued. But precaution, as a foil to preparedness, invites us to reflect with humility on the unknown unknowns, the surprises lurking beyond the imaginations of the best-trained minds that end up hurting those least able to defend themselves. How can we cultivate a systematic mindset with respect to those dangers, and can we turn humility itself into a template for more robust collective action?

If there is one lesson to draw from the recurrent crises of preparedness, it is that non-knowledge does not absolve us of responsibility for the human tragedies created by our ignorance and error. Those are the problems that the technologies of humility are specifically geared toward addressing.

The starting point for any such exercise is to be sure we are asking the best questions. Has the problem been framed in the right way? From whose viewpoints is it being observed? And are we missing a forest of non-knowing for the sparse trees of scientific knowns? In the context of a pandemic, it could well be that too rigid a focus on fighting the disease agent, the primary concern of public health experts, causes us to miss other dimensions of wider moral concern, including questions of who is most likely to be infected or die if we do not get the infection under control. In seeking to act, did we consider who was most vulnerable and how the risks would be distributed? And if not, why not?

It's not as if we could not have known. Given prior experience with health outcomes in the United States, it was not surprising that COVID-19 disproportionately affected the poor, the elderly, Blacks and Hispanics, and those living in environmentally compromised surroundings. Nor was it a shock that the dissolution of public service infrastructures—schooling, most notably—disproportionately affected women, single parents, and low-income families. Last but not least, members of these very underserved communities also proved to be most distrustful of the solutions science ultimately offered, including vaccines thrust upon groups that had historically and with good cause regarded organized medicine as their enemy. But as the GHSI, playbook, and Fineberg plan illustrate, social, political, and ethical concerns were not built into the tick boxes for what to ask and how to act that planners laid out before the pandemic escalated.

Had technologies of humility been more actively integrated into our schemes of governance and planning, we would not have missed phenomena such as vaccine hesitancy until they arrived on our doorstep as if unannounced. Where prediction runs the present out into the future, humility reverses time's arrow and pulls possible futures back to show us how to act in the present. Humility's concern is with consequences, but with special attention to the consequences of getting things wrong, leaving important viewpoints out, ignoring signs from the shadows in the certainty of having seen the light. Vaccine anxiety, after all, had been brewing for years around childhood immunization. Instead of dismissing these fears as illiterate and unscientific, and now paying the price, the technologies of humility would have asked, as some ethnographers did, why people did not trust the experts when their children's health was at stake. That inquiry would have generated a map of power and powerlessness, and of resistance at the margins, that might have informed public policy very differently. It might have queried how, precisely, to implement Fineberg's fifth injunction, to "inspire and mobilize the public." Which public, and mobilize to what ends?

There is one respect in which the technologies of humility may be less humble than the techniques of prediction. When accidents and disasters happen, policymakers often dismiss them as unintended consequences, when in fact they were merely unforeseen by those with the capacity to act. Humility rejects this easy way out. It demands that we ask in advance what new vulnerabilities might be produced by our bravest acts of preparedness, in theaters of public health, economy, environment, or war. The technologies of humility would have us reflect longer and harder on the obligations we incur when acting on imperfect knowledge, by adopting the perspectives of those who are acted upon or are themselves not able to intervene. This is the cry of Lear on the heath when, stripped down to life's bare essentials, he sees that he would have been a better king had he exposed himself "to feel what wretches feel." Humility demands just that kind of self-abnegation from power and policy: to win greater knowledge because it sees from the margins as well as the center, and deeper wisdom because it acknowledges the imperfections of human understanding.

THE CONTOURS OF IGNORANCE
Zeynep Pamuk

HUMILITY HAS NOT ALWAYS been among the popular virtues. While open-mindedness, curiosity, honesty, integrity, and perseverance are widely regarded as scientific virtues, humility is frequently left out. Nor has it enjoyed much success as a political virtue. Hume notoriously dismissed humility as a "monkish virtue," arguing that it is neither useful nor agreeable to the self or to others. By contrast, Sheila Jasanoff aims not only to revive humility as a scientific and political virtue, but to make it central to society's approach to dealing with disasters involving science and technology. An ethos of humility, she argues, is the key to dealing better with the next crisis that is sure to come.

The COVID-19 pandemic—like climate change, financial crises, hurricanes, and nuclear accidents—exposed the limits of scientific prediction and control. It was defined from the start by uncertainty, complexity, and the absence of adequate knowledge. Perhaps the one foreseeable thing was that there would be unforeseen events at every turn. Jasanoff grounds her plea for humility in the uncertainty and unpredictability that characterize such crises. The defining feature of humility, after all, is awareness of limitations—of one's knowledge and ability to gain knowledge. Humility demands that we acknowledge the likelihood of mistakes and accept the possibility of defeat rather than being confident in our predictions and capacity for control.

To evaluate the aptness of humility as a response to uncertainty and non-knowing, we must first reflect on the source of the limitations that humility would have us confront. While I agree that some inherent limitations of scientific inquiry are appropriately faced with humility, I will argue that there is another kind of limitation for which humility is at best an inadequate response and at worst a counterproductive one. Jasanoff conflates the two in her essay; my aim here is to disentangle them.

It is almost a truism that scientific knowledge is inherently uncertain, fallible, and incomplete. The sources of this uncertainty can vary. It may be due to the limits of the evidence currently available: the evidence may be flawed in some way, or the information necessary to settle a scientific dispute may simply be lacking. Uncertainty might also stem from the complexity of natural or social processes under study: causal structures might not be fully understood, or they might involve such radical uncertainty that scientists might never be able to predict them with much success. Scientists themselves are usually the first to acknowledge uncertainty and non-knowing due to these limitations. They will admit that scientific beliefs at any given time are tentative and fallible and will change when the evidence changes. In the face of these limitations, it certainly makes sense to adopt an attitude of humility. We must pay attention to the possibility of mistakes and take precautions to make them less costly.

But knowledge and understanding can be uncertain—or entirely absent—in another way, too: because of choices made about what types of knowledge should be pursued, and how. Those in a position to choose which scientific questions to ask can thereby shape what counts as significant knowledge and what can be bracketed or left out altogether. Any decision about what knowledge to pursue is also a decision about what areas of uncertainty and ignorance we can live with—whose problems we can safely ignore. In short, the limits of our knowledge and ability to control disasters do not just arise from the intrinsic limits of human powers and the complexity of natural and social systems but also from choices about where to put our limited resources of time, money, and attention. What counts as a known unknown and what remains an unknown unknown are not intrinsic facts about the world; they are endogenous to choices about the knowledge scientists and other experts have chosen to pursue in the past. As a society, our ignorance has specific contours, and those who are involved in seeking knowledge and making policy have some control over what it looks like.

Jasanoff's essay offers good examples of the kinds of knowledge that were notably absent from three major pandemic planning efforts. The Global Health Security Index model did not include variables on political polarization and trust, income inequality, racial disparities, or the marginalization of groups and regions in its calculations. The Obama administration's playbook overestimated the nation's willingness, as Jasanoff puts it, to "set aside politics and act in unison for the common good." Fineberg's call for unified command across the public and private sectors presupposed a United States that never was or had long ceased to be. All three assumed public buy-in and full compliance. Their assumptions about political unity were naïve. They did not pay enough attention to the needs of the most vulnerable communities: the poor, the elderly, Blacks, Hispanics, and Native Americans. Vaccine rollout plans did not adequately plan for vaccine hesitancy.

I could multiply the examples. Early COVID-19 models from Imperial College London and the University of Washington's Institute for Health Metrics and Evaluation, which played a crucial role in shaping the policy response in the United States and the United Kingdom, focused on short-term health outcomes and neglected the economic and social impacts of policies. They failed to take a holistic approach to health and left out the mental and physical health toll of social isolation and a severe economic downturn, increased domestic violence and substance abuse rates, delayed treatments for other diseases, and missed vaccination schedules for children. They did not consider how social behavior and interaction patterns would affect infection rates. Nor were there enough studies about how COVID-19 was affecting different population subgroups along racial, ethnic, and class lines, and the differential impacts of lockdowns and school closures.

There is a clear pattern here. In all these cases, a different kind of knowledge that would have allowed for better planning *could* have been pursued but wasn't. Consistently missing was knowledge about social and political factors; the needs of the most vulnerable communities historically neglected by science; human behavior and social interactions; a broader understanding of health, social scientific and humanistic approaches; as well as more interdisciplinary, responsive, and democratic sources of knowledge. The problem was not in the aspiration to preparedness but with a technocratic approach to preparedness that sidelined certain variables as irrelevant and ignored political realities and citizens' needs.

In responding to this second type of failing—those not inherent to science but due to negligence or bad choices—humility may not be the right solution. Emphasizing the limits of scientific knowledge and calling for humility can have the effect of absolving scientists and government officials from responsibility for failing to produce the right kind of knowledge. It can serve to excuse not knowing what was in fact knowable, and not being prepared for what we should have seen coming. It can deflect citizens' rightful criticisms by suggesting that laypeople simply fail to grasp the uncertainty and incompleteness of science. A blanket rhetoric of humility that does not distinguish between different reasons why our knowledge and capacity for control happen to be limited thus obscures the difference between limitations we could and could not have removed.

It may still be preferable to recognize and accept these limitations, but humility is not particularly useful for addressing and overcoming them. While it directs us to reflect on what we *cannot* do, it does not help us make better choices on things we *can* do. The need for humility arises when important questions have not been asked and attainable knowledge has not been pursued. This is not a state we must accept, but one we should learn from and leave behind. The more relevant virtue in preparing for the next crisis is willingness to improve, expand, and integrate our knowledge. The aim should be to produce a body of knowledge accountable to everyone, rather than responding with humility when it falls short in foreseeable ways.

Pamuk

THE LIVES OF OTHERS
Alexandre White

IN FEBRUARY 1866 the third International Sanitary Conference—an early forerunner of the World Health Organization (WHO)—convened in Constantinople at the request of the French government, bringing together representatives from more than a dozen states and empires. The pressing concern was cholera. The year before, an outbreak in Mecca had spread first into Egypt and then into Europe through Mediterranean ports. Concerned that Muslim pilgrims on hajj to Mecca might carry the disease into Egypt once again if they could return by sea, the French delegation proposed suspending all maritime traffic into and out of Arabian ports. In effect, pilgrims who did not wish to remain in Mecca would be condemned to a perilous journey across the Arabian desert and most likely death from disease or dehydration.

As historian Valeska Huber has explained, the measure was met with massive protest from Muslim delegates, who claimed that no such policy would be entertained if it were to be forced instead upon

European populations. Requisite supplies, food, and water could not possibly be distributed to tens of thousands of deserted travelers or to villagers along the coast, they pointed out: famine would be inevitable. Nor would a ban on maritime travel ensure that cholera did not spread into Egypt by land. The proposal, in short, meant risking the lives of tens of thousands of Muslims in a spurious effort to protect European lives and economic interests. Recognizing the immense loss of life at stake, chief Ottoman delegate Salih Efendi warned that "towns of living sentient beings would soon be transformed into necropoli." Despite this and other stirring objections, the measure passed. Mercifully, there was no cholera epidemic in Mecca that year, and sea travel was not suspended.

This forgotten scene from the history of medicine reverberates into the present. As the COVID-19 pandemic has made clear— both in the United States and abroad—too often our public health rationalities seek to protect some while letting others die. On this score, Sheila Jasanoff rightly calls our attention to the importance of humility in our predictive approaches and the troubling pitfalls of the world of pandemic preparedness. As Andrew Lakoff and other scholars of biosecurity have argued, the assessment of pandemic risk and the practices of infection control are fraught with contestable forms of calculation and value judgment. Jasanoff highlights the perverse chauvinism that emerges from too confidently acting upon such imperfect knowledge. I would add that these failings are not generic errors of rationality or technological hubris: they are rooted in a distinctively Western vision of a history of self-styled superiority to the rest of the world, especially when it comes to disease. To combat the casual cruelty to which this conceit gives rise, humanism must be a central component of the humility Jasanoff argues for—the understanding that the lives of others are as important and meaningful as our own. Failing to reckon with these legacies will only ensure the further creation of necropoli at home and abroad.

As Jasanoff notes, health security experts have frequently expressed concern over the expansion of global trade and travel. This fear is far from a recent preoccupation, and it has often carried connotations of the contagious other. In 1892 noted physician and early epidemiologist Adrien Proust—father of the novelist and hypochondriac Marcel—suggested in *La Défense de l'Europe Contre Le Choléra* that the rising colonization of Africa would aggravate the danger of the spread of disease to Europe, exacerbating the threat of cholera arriving from the east. The International Sanitary Conventions of the later nineteenth and early twentieth centuries, the early International Sanitary Regulations produced under the WHO, and the legally binding International Health Regulations of today all bear the same prime directive, not one of equitable health protection for all but rather "to prevent, protect against, control and provide a public health response to the international spread of disease in ways that are commensurate with and restricted to public health risks, and which avoid unnecessary interference with international traffic and trade."

In 1951, when the first regulations under the WHO were being debated, the specter of increased travel, in particular from jungle areas to other lands, projected a threat of yellow fever spread to spaces like the countries around the Indian Ocean but also North America and Europe. In 1988, after the largely triumphal twentieth-century vision of a West free from infectious disease was dashed by the devastating emergence of HIV/AIDS, Nobel-winning microbiologist Joshua Lederberg—one of the architects of a paradigm-shifting Institute of Medicine report on emerging infectious disease threats to the United States—wrote:

> The increasing density of human habitations as well as inventions such as the subway and the jet airplane that mix populations all add to the risks of spread of infection. . . . No matter how selfish our motives, we can no longer be indifferent to the suffering of others. The microbe that felled one child in a distant continent yesterday can reach yours today and seed a global pandemic tomorrow.

The logic of this appeal is telling. Its ethical force is tempered by an accommodation to self-interest: we must care about the dying child of a distant land not because her suffering is intrinsically objectionable, but because the diseases of elsewhere can easily become our own.

Jasanoff is right to note how a regime of "preparedness" has ironically produced a world of acute, rapidly accelerating crises. But we too often ignore the ways this logic is linked to a pernicious way of viewing the rest of the world as a reservoir of threatening contagion. At the same time, we elevate the protection of Western interests above others. The result is not a world unified in confronting illnesses all too capable of crossing national borders, but rather one in which the needs of the Western world are always put first.

Justifications for this regime are too often based on the supposed greater rationality and modernity of Western societies. In 2001 the chief of the U.S. Agency for International Development justified the withholding of antiretroviral therapy to Africa on the false supposition that sufficient infrastructure did not exist to refrigerate medications and that Africans "do not know what watches and clocks are," thus making routine drug taking impossible. The slowness to deliver lifesaving drugs worldwide sacrificed lives elsewhere for profit.

We are witnessing the same pattern today. Two months ago, several public health actors and committed health advocates—many of whom, such as Gregg Gonsalves and Peter Staley, have committed their lives to health care access and advocacy—protested Pfizer's and especially Moderna's refusal to license their mRNA technology to vaccine manufacturers in low- and middle-income countries. The protesters brought along a twelve-foot-high sculpture of a pile of bones—a visual representation of the necropoli we build when we elevate our own humanity above that of others.

WHY WE DON'T ACT

Jana Bacevic

WHY DO WE FAIL to predict—and even more importantly, prevent—social and political crises?

I have often had occasion to reflect on this question in my work on the dissolution of former Yugoslavia in the early 1990s. Since the 1960s, networks of scientists from both the East and the West—not to mention Yugoslav citizens themselves—had discussed and debated the future of the Socialist Federal Republic at length. Yet still most were caught off guard when events ended in Europe's bloodiest conflict since World War II. It was not that they did not have sufficient knowledge to predict this kind of future: indeed, even a few did forewarn of this possible outcome. It was rather that they could not imagine a future in which their present action was required. In this sense, the success or failure of prediction to inspire precautionary action tells us much more about ourselves than our knowledge of the world.

I see this same theme at work in Sheila Jasanoff's thoughtful analysis of precaution in the context of COVID-19. As Jasanoff notes, the pandemic is very far from not having been predicted: infectious disease experts have been warning of just such an outcome for some time. What, then, explains the inadequacy of pandemic response in the United States? Jasanoff is right to point to the limitations of a "preparedness" regime, with its distinctive approaches to global risk assessment. Yet the obstacle to better planning involves not only uncertainty regarding the objects of our knowledge, be they political parties or pathogens, but also our relationship to ourselves as knowing and acting subjects. In this sense, precautionary action rests not only on epistemic accuracy in our weighing of models and risks, but also on our affective, political, and ethical orientation to the future.

This is key to understanding the failure of prediction to prevent events such as pandemics or climate change. In these cases, failure has less to do with imperfection or uncertainty of our knowledge and more with the failure to acknowledge how our present actions are directly contributing to bringing about, or at least making more likely, certain kinds of futures—and how our actions can, and must, be changed now, today. In this sense, it is not a failure of prediction, or the failure to communicate predictions to political officials and decisionmakers, that we should worry about. Nor, from this point of view, does generic overconfidence or a lack of humility seem like a pressing problem. The culprit, as I have argued in my work on politics of knowledge and climate change, is the failure to act *before* COVID-19 or, say, 1.5° C of global warming, became the most likely futures. In these contexts, what we want to know about the future serves to obscure precisely what we do *not* want to know about the present: that we must change what we are doing, that we must behave differently.

Why do we so often prefer not to know? Classical theories of denial are not of much help here. In the context of COVID-19, very few are claiming that the virus simply does not exist or that it has been completely eradicated (even if some do deny its severity). The notion of strategic ignorance comes closer to capturing the relationship between not-knowing and not-doing: for instance, the tobacco industry's denial of the link between smoking and cancer was meant to protect their profits. In other cases, not knowing serves to avoid being held accountable later. In a recent paper, Linsey McGoey and I argue that the UK government strategically wielded ignorance in this way throughout the pandemic, interpreting scientific uncertainty about how to control coronavirus infections as a reason not to intervene. What later appeared as frantic action—installing plastic barriers, distributing sanitizing stations, implementing mandatory quarantines—obscures the government's failure to act in ways that would have rendered such action unnecessary.

Another reason we may prefer not to know—why we may prefer not to see obvious futures—is associated with the avoidance of choice. Existentialist philosophers linked it to the fear of freedom, the inevitable dizziness or lightness of being that follows when we become aware of the contingency of our lives—and our responsibility in shaping them. This anxiety-inducing awareness can be avoided in many ways, including the claim that we have no other option, that things cannot be changed. Of course, this existentialist emphasis on personal choice can easily seem misplaced—a neoliberal tool for shifting burdens onto

Bacevic

individuals, rather than pursuing structural change—but existentialists were not in the slightest bit naïve. Simone de Beauvoir, for instance, clearly emphasized that the ability of individuals to perceive themselves as free agents is shaped from the beginning by their social position, including their gender, race, class, and health. Existential ethics, she argued, requires us to act in the face of these constraints, not in spite of them.

Seen in this light, the failure to act with precaution, or the refusal to even engage in prediction, can be a way of avoiding responsibility for our actions. Like Buridan's ass, suspended between different options we claim we are too uncertain to select from, we postpone a decision until one course of action seems inevitable. While this flight from responsibility can be observed in our personal lives, it is also especially convenient for governments, which can wield strategic ignorance to maintain the status quo, all while preserving a semblance of democratic legitimacy. McGoey and I deem this sociopolitical formation "fatalistic liberalism."

Complex events, like wars or climate change, make this slippage of responsibility even easier, as it is always possible to shift between different actors as well as scales. Of course I, as an individual, cannot do anything to alter the course of climate change—it needs to be the fossil fuel companies. But of course we, the fossil fuel companies, cannot make a difference—it's the automobile industry that needs to develop cars running on sustainable sources of energy. But it's not us, pleads the automobile industry; it's governments that need to provide subsidies for renewable R&D and infrastructure. But it's not us, say the governments; it's people who must support these interventions democratically. The burden of responsibility is reliably passed around until it simply dissipates into resignation to the status quo.

In a certain sense, none of these objections is entirely wrong: the more we know about mutual determination of human and non-human elements, the more difficult it can be to shift blame onto only one group of actors. But by the same token, it can also become more difficult to deny that we all need to act now. From this vantage, the most fundamental ethical question posed by prediction is not how we can better assess whether certain events will take place; it's what we should do once it is clear they cannot be avoided.

I am not sure that humility is the best response to this question. On the contrary, what may well be required of us—whether in the face of deadly pathogens or world-destroying warming—is that we boldly and confidently fight for the futures we want to see.

Bacevic

REAPING WHAT WE SOW

Jay S. Kaufman

SHEILA JASANOFF HAS PROVIDED an expansive and nuanced rumination on our pandemic predicament, with many important insights on science, politics, and the meaning of public health preparedness. From the Maginot Line in World War II to the levees and floodwalls in New Orleans during Hurricane Katrina, history is replete with examples of fortifications and preparations that offered the appearance of precaution and readiness, only to succumb ignobly in the heat of battle. But rather than a deficiency of material integrity, Jasanoff notes, the collapse of the U.S. public health response in the face of COVID-19 owes more to the soft capacities of trust, leadership, organization, and will. The Afghan army in the summer of 2021 seemed formidable when judged by advanced weapons and numbers of soldiers but proved to be a proverbial "paper tiger" by evaporating overnight when challenged militarily. The United States' vaunted public health infrastructure suffered a similar humiliation from a rot that likewise could not be seen in tallies of personnel and material resources.

Still, I am not convinced that humility is the right focus; making the issue a matter of personality traits can distract us from the historical and material origins of our present crisis. Jasanoff appeals to classic morality tales of arrogance humbled, but these parables of comeuppance do not properly acknowledge the ideological roots of our current disaster. For example, she says of the Cuban Missile Crisis and U.S. defeat in Vietnam that these predicaments arose because "we embraced preparedness when we should have opted for precaution." But let's not forget that these crises emerged in the context of the United States extending its imperial hegemony. Can one practice empire with humility? It is even more important to bear in mind that postwar U.S. empire was an ideological struggle pitting free-market individualism against the supposed evil of communism. What made leaders like Fidel Castro and Ho Chi Minh anathema to the United States was their professed commitment to a political and economic order in which collective action was the foundation of social progress. It is exactly because of the U.S. inability to unseat their regimes that some semblance of communitarian values persists in those countries. One potential consequence is that while the United States suffered over 244 excess deaths per 100,000 population since March 2020, cumulative excess deaths have totaled only 93 per 100,000 in Vietnam and 150 per 100,000 in Cuba, despite being substantially poorer countries.

I am therefore suspicious of Jasanoff's claim that "the mistake . . . was to overestimate the certainty of our predictions and our capacity for control." Governments that have done a much better job of controlling the pandemic, including Taiwan and New Zealand, did not succeed because their officials are more humble, or less certain in their predictions.

Kaufman

I think rather that the United States reaped what it sowed, and what it sowed with such relentless fervor was a virulent opposition to social reciprocity, to any sense of a common and mutual commitment to one another as members of a shared community. Such communitarian values are exactly what are needed to weather the storm of a pandemic, to work with collective purpose and a sense of shared vulnerability and mutual respect. The simple truth is that the United States has a weak ideological commitment to public health exactly because it is *public*. The U.S. Achilles's heel is not lack of humility; it is a toxic social ideology rooted in a blind obsession with individual freedom.

Another key moment in the U.S. war against communal commitments arose in the backlash to the victories of the civil rights movement. By the middle of the twentieth century, the United States had generated a vast infrastructure of public spaces, amenities, and institutions, including schools, universities, hospitals, parks, and swimming pools. The response across the country but especially in the South was to eviscerate these facilities rather than share them across the color line; what followed was an explosion of privatized institutions and services. For the last forty years, U.S. neoliberalism has steadily eroded public goods in the name of individual liberty. As an outlier among rich countries for its low social investment—including its lack of universal health care—the United States was uniquely positioned to flub any important public health challenge.

In this climate of relentless assault on the collective, it is not surprising that the United States also lacks shared values. Jasanoff's discussion of the precautionary principle focuses on uncertainty over risks, but the real problem is profound disagreement over values. Suppose we have some metric of human thriving. Is it better to aim for this measure to be as high as possible on average, or should we prefer instead to minimize the risk of anyone falling below some critical lower value? Answering this question requires a value judgment. What explains the difference in pandemic response between, say, Germany and Texas is not differing levels of certainty about how to act but a fundamental disagreement about priorities. Jasanoff points to the governors of Florida and Texas who "went to war against their own cities and school districts to prevent masking orders for students from taking effect." Contrasting this with Harvey Fineberg's editorial from April 2020, she suggests that this is "not exactly a picture of efficient, centralized high command in action." Except that it is. It is just that the governors of Florida and Texas have a very different set of priorities and values from those that Jasanoff embraces.

Pandemics are fundamentally problems of collective action: infection is a shared risk, not a private one. My risk of disease is lowered when you are vaccinated, and vice versa. Everyone's fate is in everyone else's hands. Jasanoff references this fact when she notes that "securing public health and public safety requires human beings to give up aspects of their liberty in the interests of a common good." But again, the problem is that we don't agree on this priority, not that we are too certain in our evaluations of risk.

The root of "humility" means "of the earth," and I agree with Jasanoff that we could all do better to stay grounded, conscious of our humble natures, fragilities, and interdependence. Yet this injunction should not blind us to the more pressing challenge we are up against. There has been a relentless ideological war, beating ruthlessly against any vestiges of collectivism that might linger in our hearts, pulling

Kaufman

people apart from one another and thus making them vulnerable to exactly this crisis. The human toll has been horrendous, but in the United States, it is just the cost of doing business. Changing that will require a political movement, not just a better attitude.

FINAL RESPONSE
Sheila Jasanoff

I AM GRATEFUL to the four readers who engaged with my essay for their careful attention, and also for showing me inadvertently how it failed to make its mark. I first put the phrase "technologies of humility" into circulation in 2003. The "technologies" I support are not, as my essay observes, merely a mental state—"a stance of modesty vis-à-vis the powerful and still poorly understood forces of nature and society"—but rather a set of "institutional mechanisms" designed to incorporate "memory, experience, and concerns for justice into our schemes of governance and public policy." The humility I advocate is thus not a personal attitude but rather a collective practice of societal self-reflection aimed at understanding why we persistently repeat the same kinds of mistakes, overestimating our power to control futures as yet in-the-making.

This is precisely the distinction that Zeynep Pamuk charges me with conflating, but her own comments suggest an imperfect understanding of the ways in which the regime of preparedness makes U.S. decisionmakers impervious to their own blind spots. Knowledge, Pamuk says, can be incomplete not only because of what we do not yet know, but also "because of choices made about what types of knowledge should be pursued, and how." Indeed! The first rule of policy is that one must frame a problem right in order to find the right facts and come to the right conclusions. My aim is to call attention to the manifold points at which well-intentioned policymakers, well-prepared for the "coming plague," failed to assess what I have called the "politics of public health." Instead of worrying about the political context into which their decisions would land, they repeatedly focused on closing gaps in our scientific knowledge of how pandemics arise and spread. As recently as January 2021, Margaret Hamburg, one of the nation's most prominent public health experts, said in a public forum that we had failed because of insufficient "efforts to identify critical gaps in knowledge that would affect the contours and control measures for this pandemic." Her emphasis was on more biological knowledge and better management, not absence of political understanding and resulting lack of control.

Jana Bacevic is correct in her assertion that "the success or failure of prediction to inspire precautionary action tells us much more about ourselves than our knowledge of the world." From that starting point, however, she veers into an analysis that focuses on strategic ignorance and responsibility avoidance as explanations for why we choose not to know what would guard us against error. That analysis ascribes both bad faith and too much agency to public health officials and other decisionmakers—a position for which I see little evidence in this crisis. Bacevic concludes that, from her viewpoint, neither "generic overconfidence or a lack of humility seem like a pressing problem." But she misunderstands the systemic nature of the knowledge deficits that societies fall into when choosing between courses of action. As I have argued elsewhere, there are deep-seated, systematic, institutional commitments to ways of knowing—*civic epistemologies* as I call them—that consistently demote some kinds of knowledge at the expense of others. For Americans, this results in an over-valuation of predictive, technical knowledge in relation to insights from history, sociology and politics. The three predictive exercises analyzed in my essay all exemplify that lack of self-awareness, and all point to the dangers of, in Bacevic's words, "boldly and confidently fight[ing] for the futures we want to see."

Alexandre White, in contrast to Bacevic, underscores the risks of coupling boldness of vision to bad motives in his historically sensitive account of the West's "pernicious way of viewing the rest of the world as a reservoir of threatening contagion." But he surely goes too far in attributing the multiple and dispersed policy errors of the pandemic to "a distinctively Western vision of a history of self-styled superiority to rest of the world, especially when it comes to disease." A closely investigated comparative study I am co-leading of national approaches to COVID-19 policies disclosed no such monolithic "Western vision." The U.S. self-understanding of a technologically superior society, able to cure any ill with a well-timed technological fix, has to be sure enjoyed wide currency in the post-colonial world, but that technocratic vision is precisely what needs to be shaken in the aftermath of the pandemic, with a turn toward humility as I suspect White would agree.

Jasanoff

Jay Kaufman misconstrues humility as "a matter of personality traits" or "a better attitude" rather than as a call for different institutional commitments and practices as discussed in my essay. I am, however, heartened that he then whole-heartedly embraces the playbook from my 2003 article, as well as a half-century of other writing on risk and regulation by scholars in my field of science and technology studies. I could not agree more with his assessment that the disasters leading to our own sad "necropoli" (to borrow White's term) can be traced to a "virulent opposition to social reciprocity, to any sense of a common and mutual commitment to one another as members of a shared community." Indeed, in our comparative study and elsewhere, colleagues and I have repeatedly emphasized the absence of mechanisms for generating, even temporarily, a sense of a common purpose in the United States, the very failing that Kaufman also bewails. Harvey Fineberg, a renowned public health intellectual, assumed that the U.S. federal government would be able to draw the nation together in ten weeks. The gubernatorial actions in Florida and Texas, among others, demonstrate that his confidence was misplaced. We need to revisit that territory of failed calls to action with due humility about the limits of our expertise, our wisdom, and our capacity to unite in times of national crisis.

Big societal failures of self-awareness are self-inflicted wounds that can be traced, I argue, to the habitual ways in which we normally generate collective knowledge. All four respondents recognize this problem, but they do not take further steps to ask how we got there or, having done so, how we might become wiser the next time around. The technologies of humility I propose would require us to improve our skills of *normative* forecasting: to ask whether we framed our questions right; to draw in marginalized and uncomfortable viewpoints; to review our history of crises with less triumphalist eyes; and always to identify who is most vulnerable if we go wrong, and who would bear the costs.

I invite others to take up this conversation, knowing that the answers to our most critical problems may lie in zones where our collective, deeply institutionalized, and culturally trained habits of thought do not easily allow us to roam: where, as T. S. Eliot suggested in what could be read as a plea for technologies of humility, things are:

Not known, because not looked for
But heard, half-heard, in the stillness
Between two waves of the sea.

ESSAYS

ESSAYS

IMAGINE THE WORST
Oded Na'aman

WE ARE FINE, for now. What to do with the prospect of future ruin? The question seems to bring our end ever so closer. Try to think about other things. Look outside. Listen to your breath. Read a book. Work. Watch television. Look online for something. Is it better to be oblivious? Don't answer this question. Work. Go for a run. Tweet something. Post something. Wait for reactions. Be with friends. Make a drink. Listen to your breath. Work. Look at the sky. We are fine.

Do we have a problem? Do we worry too much? Do we need treatment? Or is it the other way around? Do we have a problem because we don't worry *enough*? If we could only work up the courage to face the threat, whatever form it takes, then we might have a chance to prevent or forestall it. We'd be ready. But no. No, even the thought that we can do something is an illusion. A little more or less time wouldn't make a difference in the grand scheme of things. There is nothing we can do about it. No matter when, the end will come too soon. But what about now? Why can't we at least be alive now? We imagine how it will happen. When we ignore it, we feel it lurking, stalking us. We have a problem. We need help. Our mind can't deal with this on its own. Our imagination torments us with visions of reality.

For us inhabiting the modern world, psychologists and psychiatrists are the doctors of the mind. But according to Cicero, we should turn instead to philosophy. Unlike the medical science of the body, Cicero says, philosophy is self-administered: "the help of philosophy is something we need not look to others to gain." But in what sense are we our own healers if we rely on philosophers to teach us? And why should we listen to philosophers in the first place—do they really fare any better than we do? Seneca offers the following confession in his *Letters on Ethics to Lucilius*:

> "How is it that you are advising me?" you say. "Have you already advised yourself? Have you got yourself straightened out? . . . I am not such a hypocrite as to offer cures while I am sick myself. No, I am lying in the same ward, as it were, conversing with you about our common ailment and sharing remedies. So listen to me as if I were talking to myself: I am letting you into my private room and giving myself instructions while you are standing by.

Philosophers don't have answers, philosophy does. Moreover, philosophy's answers are more than conclusions backed by arguments, they are movements and habits of thought. Philosophy is an activity, a daily exercise of the mind, a conversation with others that is also a conversation with oneself. So understood, philosophical theses are forms of address: they are said or written *by* someone *to* someone (though sometimes both are the same person). Their meaning cannot be properly understood when abstracted from the circumstances of their occurrence.

Ambivalence is built into this model of philosophy. It is a mistake to try to disentangle the abstract from the concrete, content from style, word from deed. Philosophical thinking is an attempt to rescue the mind from its own trappings; to philosophize is to seek the way when one is lost. Those who make grand, universal, and decisive philosophical claims—about reason, rationality, or truth—are often those whose lives are in disarray. This is not to say that such claims must be insincere nor is it to cast doubt on their veracity. Rather, the fact that universal philosophical claims are always made by individual people with particular longings and fears means that such claims express much more than they let on. Their meaning extends beyond their explicit content. It is with this in mind that we can turn to philosophy for help.

Ancient Self-Help

THE ANCIENTS BELIEVED that philosophy could teach us how to live in the face of our inevitable ruin. But they were of two minds: some, with Epicurus, thought that we should look away from future suffering and misfortune while others, with the Stoics, thought that we should fix our gaze on the evils that await us. We find both approaches in Seneca; sometimes he appeals to one, sometimes to the other. In Letter 24 he writes to Lucilius:

> You write that you are worried about the outcome of a lawsuit that an enemy's rage has brought against you. You suppose that I will urge you to fix your thoughts on the best and to ease your mind with comforting expectations. After all, what need is there to take an advance on future troubles, ruining the present with fear of the future? When troubles come is time enough to bear them. Surely it is foolish to be miserable now just because you are going to be miserable later on! But what I will do is lead you down a different road to tranquility. If you want to be rid of worry, then fix your mind on whatever it is that you are afraid might happen as a thing that definitely will happen. Whatever bad event that might be, take the measure of it mentally and so assess your fear. You will soon realize that what you fear is either no great matter or not long lasting.

Seneca recommends here a favorite method of the Stoics. Cicero calls it *praemeditatio futurorum malorum*: "the prerehearsal of future evils." Cicero attributes the method to Anaxagoras, who, upon hearing of his son's death, is claimed to have said: "I knew my child was mortal." Anaxagoras's pupil, Euripides, the great Greek tragedian, puts the following speech in the mouth of Theseus: "I pondered in my heart the miseries / to come / . . . so that if by chance / some one of them should happen, I'd not be / unready, not torn suddenly with pain." Initially this peculiar exercise, focusing on our future plight, might seem to indulge our anxiety rather than calm it. We might therefore be inclined to agree with Epicurus, who, according to Cicero, rejected the method and instead recommended distracting the mind from suffering and redirecting it to pleasures. Cicero, however, sides with the Stoics:

> Nothing does so much to soften the impact of distress as this practice of thinking at all times that there is no misfortune that cannot befall us. . . . The result is not that we are always sad, but that we are never sad at all. A person is not saddened by thinking about the nature of things, about the changefulness of life and the weakness of humankind; rather, it is in this, above all, that one gains the benefits of wisdom.

The prerehearsal of future evils is supposed to help us in three interrelated ways. First, by contemplating future misfortunes we avoid being surprised by them, and this, it is thought, dilutes their impact. Seneca gives voice to this idea when he writes: "When one is unprepared for a disaster, it has a greater effect: shock intensifies the blow. No mortal can fail to grieve more deeply when amazement is added to the loss." Thus, through *praemeditatio* we disabuse ourselves of the illusion of security and a false sense of immunity. Loss is always near and often random, sudden, and swift.

The second benefit of reflecting on future evils is that it normalizes loss and suffering as necessary and human. Cicero writes that "one understands that troubles are part of human life, and that to endure them, as we must, is also human." Suffering does not single us out; on the contrary, through suffering we experience our humanity. Seneca adds that since suffering is everyone's lot, we have no grounds for complaint, writing "we should pay without complaint the taxes of our morality." Recognizing that suffering is inevitable and ubiquitous is meant to help us accept it. Euripides, cited by Cicero, writes: "No

Na'aman

mortal lives who is untouched by grief / and sickness. Many have to bury children / and bear new ones; death is ordained for all. / And humans feel anxiety for this—in vain: / earth must return to earth, and life for all / be mowed, like wheat. Necessity insists."

But how does the necessity of suffering provide any comfort? Cicero considers this point as well: isn't "the fact that we are subject to such cruel necessity . . . itself a reason to grieve[?]" He replies that such thought is a form of vanity. We are not gods; by accepting suffering, we accept our humanity. Instead of clinging to the false hope that we will be spared and lamenting our fate when our time to suffer inevitably arrives, we must take inspiration from others who have endured loss and suffering with grace. While outrage exacerbates our suffering, acceptance lessens it. Seneca recommends the following internal dialogue between oneself and one's pain: "You are only pain, whom that arthritic fellow there despises, whom the dyspeptic endures at fancy meals, whom the merest girl endures in childbirth."

The final benefit of contemplating future misfortunes is that one realizes that these events are not evil. Anything that Fortune can take from us, Seneca says, cannot contribute to happiness: "the happy life consists solely in perfecting our rationality; for perfected rationality is the one thing that keeps the spirit high and takes a stand against fortune." Reason is invulnerable to contingencies and mishaps. Thus, by identifying with reason, we immunize ourselves against loss. Only by rehearsing future evils can we accomplish virtuous identification with reason and come to see evils as insignificant. In fact, Cicero says, we learn from this method of reason what we learn from the experience of grief as it diminishes with time: "gradually over time the pain grows less . . . because experience teaches us the lesson reason ought to have taught, that what seemed so serious is not in reality very significant."

The prerehearsal of future evils is thus an exercise in loosening our attachments and identifications, and undoing our love for particular people and places. Pierre Hadot describes stoic practices as "a movement of conversion toward the self" that is also a movement toward "a new way of being-in-the-world, which consists in becoming aware of oneself as a part of nature, and a portion of universal reason."

Should we accept this aspiration to disown our attachments to anything that can be lost? It is difficult, for example, to accept Cicero's claim that the loss of our loved ones is not worth grieving. But it is here that we must remember the ambivalence of the ancients' philosophical thought. We should not separate Cicero's claim about the insignificance of loss from the circumstances in which it was conceived and written. He was in the grip of grief when writing the *Tusculanae Disputationes*, the work in which these claims appear. His only daughter, Tullia, whom he adored, died soon after giving birth to his first grandchild.

In his personal letters from that time, Cicero tells of the violent anguish that took over: the wish to be alone, long walks in the woods, and uncontrollable fits of weeping. "Reading and writing do not comfort me but they do distract me," he writes. In fact, he held on to his pain: "I try in every way I can to repair my countenance—though not my heart. I think sometimes that I am wrong to do so, at other times that I will be wrong not to." He embarked on a writing frenzy. Among the various works he wrote in the months following his daughter's death was *Consolation*, "which I composed in the midst of sorrow and pain, not being a wise person myself. I . . . applied a remedy to the mind's swelling while it was still fresh. I brought the force of nature to bear upon it, so that my great pain would give way to the greatness of the medicine."

Like Seneca, Cicero was philosophizing to heal himself. What initially appears as Cicero's heartless dismissal of the significance of loss is, in fact, the cry of a bereaved father and a distressed mind desperately trying to find its bearings. When philosophy is at once a reasoned investigation of eternal truths and a practice of self-help—a theory and a conversation—even the most decisive philosophical statement is steeped in ambivalence.

In rehearsing future evils Cicero was also rehearsing past ones, but the question he poses is neither about the future nor the past. Rather, he asks: What, if anything, should ruin us? Is abject and eternal grief ever called for? This is not a matter of *how* to avoid the pain of loss, but whether we have *reason* to feel it at all. The answer to the question determines, at once, our relation to past *and* future evils. It is understandable that we should want to be justified in seeking relief, especially when loss casts its shadow over us. But do we really lack reason to be anguished by loss? An affirmative answer would be comforting for us only if true. Indeed, the Stoics believed that an affirmative answer is true—we lack reason for grief—and that we must use our imagination to see this truth.

The Stoic answer is, I believe, mistaken. There are some things to which any decent, loving person must respond with anguish and horror. But the Stoic idea that we come to know things for what they really are only through imagination strikes me as both profound and perplexing.

Doesn't imagination lead us astray? Isn't imagination the reason we project onto reality our own fears and desires, and fail to see it for what it is? Imagination can certainly deceive us, the Stoics would agree, but only when we let it run wild. When properly executed, the prerehearsal of future evils subjects imagination to the dictum of reason and the authority of the rational will. It thereby exposes as "indifferent"—that is, as neither good nor bad—that which initially appeared to be evil. When exercised virtuously, our imagination helps subdue the mind's demons and deny external reality the force it often has over us. The Stoics also advise that imagination must be practiced and developed. We must work to expand it and imagine truthfully, without distorting the imagined object according to our wishes or fears. We cannot avoid the dread of future evils by ceasing to imagine them altogether, but neither should we let our imagination bring our anxieties to life.

The Stoics were optimists not merely because they thought that a virtuous person cannot suffer evil and loss, but also because they thought that our imagination has no limits. If we work at it, they believed, we can imagine the worst that might possibly happen to us—if we truthfully consider every possible evil, nothing can shock us, merit our indignation, or hurt us. We will be fine.

Imagining the Unimaginable

THIS IS NOT just about death. We are not merely terrified by our future demise; we are terrified by the demise of what we love. We are terrified of living in an empty world, a world that has been gutted. There are disasters we do not wish to survive; changes we do not want to endure. Some things are *supposed* to destroy us, but they might not. The prospect of surviving such loss is a source of terror. By imagining future evils, we contemplate our present separateness from what we love. Our terror is a form of revolt: in the name of love, we refuse to imagine.

In *Year of Magical Thinking* (2005) Joan Didion writes about the death of her husband, John, and her refusal to imagine her life without him. Though she knows on some level that he is gone, she cannot believe it. In denying reality, she resorts to what she calls "magical thinking": somehow John will return home and wear his clothes again, need his shoes again, and sit in his chair again. She cannot imagine John's death. Of course, Didion *knows* John is dead, but she doesn't believe it in the way one believes something to be real. It may seem strange, but recognizing something as real requires imagining it as such. The sheer fact of reality is not enough.

Where, then, does Stoic imagination lead us? For all its concern with reality and truth, Stoicism lends itself to avoidance. When Cicero denies the significance of loss and the appropriateness of grief, he denies reality. Like Didion, he exercises magical thinking, refusing to imagine the very worst, that his only daughter, whose existence gave his life a sense of meaning, is gone. He would rather imagine that she was never as important to him as his grief suggests: "What seemed so serious is not in reality very significant." Cicero does not deny reality by denying the event of his daughter's death; he denies reality by denying her death as a *loss*. Thus, in his Stoic proclamations, Cicero reveals the shortcomings of imagination. It is easier for him to imagine that no one could be so important as to merit the anguish of grief than to imagine that Tullia, the most important thing in his life, is gone forever. When stared at long enough, Stoicism begins to look like nihilism.

But we should not judge Cicero too harshly. Some form of magical thinking seems to be *called for* when a loved one dies. It is an obligation of love and devotion to resist the idea that life will continue without someone we love deeply. Though we want our loved ones to live on after we are gone, we would be bothered by the thought that they might continue with their lives without missing a beat. We do not want to be lost without a fight. Yet the same love and devotion also requires recognition of the loss and its significance. "I knew my child was mortal," said Anaxagoras, the Stoics' hero. Perhaps this means that to appreciate those we love, we must also appreciate the wonder, brevity, and finitude of their existence. The certainty of future loss is at the heart of love, it breathes life into it and makes even the dullest moments count. Love issues conflicting commandments: hold on; let go. As in philosophical thought, so in the space between us and those closest to us we find an ineradicable ambivalence.

That various things are simultaneously imaginable and unimaginable is essential to love, our sense of self, and our sense of what is real. When we fantasize about a different life—with a different husband or wife, different parents or children, in a different part of the world, with a different language and climate—we normally cannot imagine our fantasy *as reality*. That is, we indulge in the fantasy as such; we enjoy it from a distance.

Na'aman

Take the movie theater as an example: we find relief from our lives and the present moment by giving ourselves to the drama, tragedy, suspense, or horror that is projected on the screen. We can do this because in the darkness of the movie theater we feel safe from the fantasy in which we are immersed. A movie might be a perfect depiction of reality, yet if we remain aware of our position in relation to what it depicts, we do not mistake it for reality (the serial killer is on the loose, but we are never his potential victims; the Titanic is sinking, but we will not drown). This is true of fiction and of art in general—a sense of safety, of distance, is a condition for the most engrossing fantasies.

However, if we imagine the fantasy-life as a real possibility, as something we might choose given the chance or something we might endure, then real life often becomes harder to sustain. It is a phenomenon many of us are familiar with: the closer the fantasy seems to us, the less we can accept reality. At the extreme, we become estranged from the people in our life and from ourselves. When real life becomes unimaginable *as reality*, we witness it as if from a point of view outside of it—from a movie theatre in another world. From this external position, nonsensical thoughts become meaningful: Is this who I am? Is this how I live?

Sometimes a person might experience something so at odds with her sense of reality that she is thereafter trapped in another world. In *The Great War and Modern Memory* (1975), Paul Fussell explains soldiers' tendency to experience war as "unreal." He writes: "it is impossible for a participant to believe that he is taking part in such murderous proceedings in his own character. The whole thing is too grossly farcical, perverse, cruel, and absurd to be credited as a form of 'real life.'" To have a real sense of the experience of war is to have a sense of the experience of war as unreal. Fussell gives an example from Stuart Cloete's *How Young They Died* (1969), a novel about World War I, in which Jim Hilton, wounded, makes his way to the rear:

> The curious thing was that he was not here; he was somewhere else. On a high place . . . looking down at this solitary figure picking its way between the shell holes. He thought: that's young Captain Jim Hilton, that little figure. I wonder if he'll make it. . . . He was an observer, not a participant. It was always like that in war though he had not realized it before. You were never you. The I part of you was somewhere else.

The experience of the war does not end with the war. One is stuck in the experience precisely because one does not recognize oneself in it. The unreality of the war spreads to other areas of one's life, until everything is colored by events one cannot recall but can't help remembering. One remains always in exile, "somewhere else," never oneself.

But even those of us fortunate enough to find reality imaginable still need to imagine other worlds to preserve our sense of the real. Our fantasies, while expressing real desires and frustrations, often reach for things we do not really want. Or we do really want them—perhaps even desperately want them—but we don't want them to be real.

This distance from fantasy also allows us to contemplate our fears. In an essay about tragedy and its importance to moral thought,

Bernard Williams writes that there are evils that can only be acknowledged in fiction: "When . . . [Nietzsche] said that we have art so that we do not perish from the truth, he did not mean that we use art in order to escape from the truth: he meant that we have art so that we can both grasp the truth and not perish from it." Truths we cannot bear in reality, we can often confront in fiction. In art we rehearse evils that we cannot—and perhaps should not—imagine as real. The ambivalence of imagination, like the ambivalence of philosophical thought, makes truthfulness possible even when truth can barely be fathomed.

Imagining Evils

WE ARE TORMENTED by imaginations of past and future evils. So we try to avoid them by distracting ourselves or convincing ourselves that they are smaller than they are—that they need not concern us. These maneuvers go only so far. Unless we descend into madness and avoid reality altogether, we must sense the presence of things that our loves and attachments forbid us from imagining. Past and future evils torment us because they are at once *real* (because the world is as it is and human beings are as they are) and *impossible* (because we stand to lose everything, or because everything has already been lost and we are still here).

Yet we must acknowledge the reality of evils because denying them might lead us, with Cicero, to deny the value of the people and things we cannot imagine losing. To deny that Tullia's death is a loss is to deny that Tullia's life was precious; it is to deny Tullia and those who loved her. For Cicero, it is also self-denial. Like the mouse in Franz Kafka's "A Little Fable" (1931), we change direction to escape the trap, but run straight into the cat's mouth. Avoidance consumes us.

Shakespeare's *King Lear* is an exploration of this predicament and its horrifying implications. Like Cicero, King Lear disowns his daughter, Cordelia, the person he loves best, while she is still alive. Stanley Cavell, in his essay "The Avoidance of Love: A reading of *King Lear*" (2015), writes that Lear's dominating motivation is to avoid being recognized. To avoid his love for Cordelia, Lear humiliates her; to avoid the shame of his betrayal, Lear avoids himself and the world. Descending into madness, Lear asks: "Who is it that can tell me who I am?" The Fool replies: "Lear's shadow."

Cavell writes of this exchange:

> Suppose the Fool has precisely answered Lear's question, which is only characteristic of him. Then his reply means: Lear's shadow can tell you who you are. If this is heard, it will mean that the answer to Lear's question is held in the inescapable Lear which is now obscure and obscuring, and in the inescapable Lear which is projected upon the world, and that Lear is double and has a double . . . [the play] taunts the characters with their lack of wholeness, their separation from themselves, by loss or denial or opposition.

In fiction, in art, we find a space between the real and the impossible where we may rehearse evils—a space where we can recognize ourselves in our doubles and be recognized by others. Ambivalence, it turns out, is a path to a place where the mind can roam free, safe from reality, studying itself and the world it occupies by studying other minds and worlds. "We are double in ourselves," Michel de Montaigne wrote, "we believe what we disbelieve, and we cannot rid ourselves of what we condemn." We are not fine. Yet here we are.

RISK SOCIETY

Caley Horan

IN 1914, ON THE EVE OF WORLD WAR I, philosopher Josiah Royce celebrated the utopian promise of insurance. In an address delivered at the University of California, Berkeley, Royce welcomed what he called "the coming social order of the insurer"—a new system of global governance based on the model of mutual insurance. Building on the work of fellow philosopher Charles Sanders Peirce, Royce imagined on the horizon a global "community of insurance" made up of all the nations of the world.

Under this new system, Royce predicted, every nation would contribute to a large insurance pool overseen by an independent world body. The result would not only insure the peoples of the world against future disasters, natural and manmade. It would also help bring them closer together by encouraging a spirit of interdependence and mutual aid—a "genuine community of mankind" that would contribute "to peace, to loyalty, to social unity, to active charity, as no other community of interpretation has ever done."

Forty years later, U.S. science fiction authors Frederik Pohl and Lester del Rey imagined a vastly different insurance future. Their 1955 novel *Preferred Risk* depicts a dystopian insurance era ruled by "The Company," a massive insurance firm that achieves total global domination, displacing state governments. The Company rises to power by distributing insurance for everything imaginable: hunger, natural disasters, reproduction, war. It rules over humanity by refining every action and consequence down to a scale of precise probabilities, represented in complex actuarial tables decipherable only by experts. Most people embrace the new era, despite being permanently segregated into risk classes that dictate what they eat, where they live, how they work, and who they meet. Others struggle simply to survive. A desperate group of outcasts—the "uninsurables"—live miserably on the outskirts of society, shunned as deviants by those lucky enough to be classified as "preferred risks."

Neither of these accounts successfully predicted the course insurance would take in the United States over the twentieth century, which was defined instead by complex relationships between private corporations and the state. But taken together, these two visions reveal the range of possibilities inherent in insurance as a system of social governance. Decades before sociologists and legal scholars spoke of "insurance as governance," Royce imagined insurance as a powerful form of social and political organization. More than a risk-spreading mechanism, he argued, it could also function as a powerful mode of governance, a form of association capable of shaping social understandings of responsibility and dictating relationships between individuals and groups. Yet Royce failed to predict the forces that would oppose the collective nature of insurance and seek to privatize the management of risk and the provision of security. Instead, *Preferred Risk* proved eerily prescient. From the omnipresence of corporate-controlled data to the plight of "uninsurables" and the risk classification schemes that severely limit access to social goods, Pohl and del Rey's dystopian vision mirrors our own insurance era in striking ways.

Those dystopian elements are increasingly facing resistance. Calls to check the power of private insurers and more equally distribute access to security have multiplied over the past decade. Gallup polling, for example, shows a steady and significant uptick since 2010 in U.S. support for replacement of private health insurance with a government-run system—support that has reached levels unseen since the 1940s. As we think about how to imagine new insurance futures, we will have to reckon, in particular, with two broad features of insurance provision in the United States: the fraught relationship between the private insurance industry and the state, and the growing power of insurance companies in gathering and wielding data about individuals and groups. Each presents unique obstacles to the more utopian possibilities Royce envisioned.

THE U.S. INSURANCE INDUSTRY has developed a complex relationship with the state—one that both works to the industry's advantage and obstructs efforts for reform. Though industry leaders have often expressed fears of government intrusion (whether by competition or regulation), partnerships with government became increasingly desirable for the industry as it grew rapidly after World War II. Many large insurers even welcomed the landmark creation of Medicare and Medicaid in 1965, the first major expansion of the U.S. welfare state since the 1930s. Under these programs insurance companies became primary managers and coordinators of medical services, overseeing a government-funded safety net designed to catch Americans deemed too risky for the private health insurance market.

The burden of providing security for these "bad risks" now fell to federal and state governments, leaving private insurance companies with a consumer base less likely to make claims and less costly to insure. This partnership, the lynchpin of America's public private health insurance system, did not challenge the viability or profits of the private insurance industry. In fact, as historian Christy Ford Chapin argues, it helped legitimize the previously contested private insurance model—neutralizing, at least for a time, calls for universal insurance programs that would cover all Americans.

Partnerships in which commercial insurers in other fields worked with or subcontracted for government became common by the 1970s. Laws requiring private insurance coverage before driving a car or buying a home, for example, granted the insurance industry immense power to shape the lives of Americans and determine who had the ability to maintain property and build wealth. Critics of these laws and other insurance practices faced serious obstacles, including a powerful insurance lobby and a state-based regulatory system that made reform on a national level nearly impossible. The

1945 McCarran–Ferguson Act cemented this state-based system, which exempted insurance from federal regulation, including most antitrust abuses—a major reason social movements led by civil rights and feminist activists in the 1970s and 1980s failed to achieve substantial and lasting reform on the federal level. The insurance industry has fought aggressively over the past seventy-six years to protect McCarran–Ferguson.

State-level consumer activists did eventually succeed in passing strong insurance regulations. In California, for example, a consumer movement supported by Ralph Nader successfully advocated for Proposition 103, passed in 1988. The law required property and casualty insurers to scale back premiums by 20 percent and to seek approval from the California Department of Insurance before setting rates. These reforms saved auto insurance consumers in the state over $100 billion between 1989 and 2013. While other states have attempted to pass similar reforms since the late 1980s, none has succeeded in establishing regulations as far reaching as those in California—in part because of increased pressure from insurance lobbyists. After Prop 103 passed, the industry organized nationally to head off similar legislation in other states, hiring specialized public relations firms and calling on local officials to reject new calls for regulation.

This fraught history of reform has led to enduring social inequities. Despite this victory on premiums, for example, California's efforts did not eradicate the racial divide in insurance access and pricing that persists across the nation to this day. A groundbreaking *ProPublica* study in 2017 found that California drivers who resided in minority neighborhoods still paid over 10 percent more for auto insurance than drivers with "similar risk" living in zip codes that were primarily white. In states such as Missouri and Illinois, drivers living in primarily minority zip codes paid as much as 30 percent more for insurance than drivers residing in majority-white zip codes.

Such inequalities are deeply imbedded in insurance practice and have been intensified by partnerships with government that prioritize corporate interests over both consumer rights and the social good. As numerous failed efforts to combat insurance discrimination have shown, rampant inequalities in private insurance provision cannot be eliminated by state-level regulation alone. Federal regulation that addresses insurance as a social issue—not simply a consumer one—is needed in order to eradicate systemic inequalities historically baked into insurance marketing, underwriting, pricing, and classification structures.

Yet attempts to repeal McCarran–Ferguson have achieved little success over the past half century, despite calls for reform from consumer rights groups and professional organizations in other industries. These efforts led the United States House of Representatives to pass in 2017 a bill that would haved repealed McCarran–Ferguson. After aggressive lobbying by the insurance industry, the bill failed to pass in the Senate—a pattern insurance critics have witnessed repeatedly over the past several decades. If future reformers hope to change the regulatory structure that governs the industry, they will need to develop tools capable of restraining the insurance lobby, while also attracting support from a public that remains largely ignorant of insurance law and its impact on the lives of most Americans.

Efforts to educate the public about insurance practice and regulation over the past half century have achieved the most success regarding health insurance. The 2010 Patient Protection and Affordable Care Act (ACA) marked a turning point in public discourse surrounding both health care and insurance provision in the United States. During the months leading up to the act's passage, Americans encountered detailed discussions of premium rating structures, exclusions based on preexisting conditions, financing of long-term care coverage, and other aspects of insurance practice and policy. Though the final version of the act failed to secure universal health coverage (a primary goal of many proponents), it did significantly reduce the number of uninsured Americans under age 65—from more than 44 million in 2013 (the year before most of its requirements went into effect) to just below 27 million in 2016. This reduction was made possible by expanding Medicaid to cover more low-income Americans; by the creation of market exchanges through which qualifying individuals and businesses could purchase subsidized insurance plans; and through regulations preventing private insurers from charging higher premiums or denying coverage to individuals with preexisting conditions.

But millions still lack coverage or struggle to pay high premiums and copays. This is true especially in states that have opted out of the ACA's federal funding for Medicaid expansion. Though the expansion was intended to be national, a 2012 Supreme Court ruling made it optional for states, leading many Republican-controlled state legislatures to reject expansion. Between 2016 and 2018, these states—many of which are located in the South and are home to large numbers of low-income people of color—witnessed a significant increase in uninsured residents, while states that accepted expansion saw a decrease.

These disparities, and many of the ACA's basic features, represent a continuation of historical trends toward privatization—not the departure from the past claimed by proponents hesitant to embrace more sweeping change. The enthusiasm of ACA architects for "market-based solutions," exemplified by the creation of online insurance exchanges, extends decades-old industry efforts to expand private markets and limit public options. Joel Ario, director of the Office of Health Insurance Exchanges under President Barack Obama, argued that one of the key goals of the ACA was to replace the "welfare model" of health care provision with an industry-based "insurance model." Ezekiel Emanuel, Obama's special adviser on health care reform during the years the ACA was developed, shared this sentiment, arguing in 2014 that market exchanges would eventually produce an "Amazon-like" shopping experience that would generate "positive branding" and ultimately replace both public insurance and employer group plans.

Despite these limitations, Americans have welcomed the act's preexisting conditions ban and accepted the notion that access to health care should not be restricted to those with favorable risk ratings. As of 2020, 63 percent of Americans polled by the Pew Research Center believed that it is "the federal government's responsibility to make sure all Americans have health care coverage." A reinvigorated and growing belief that health care is a human right—one that should not be contingent on the ability of corporations to make profits—stands to fundamentally reshape the relationship between private insurance and the state.

ANOTHER TROUBLING FEATURE of insurance provision today is the insurance industry's increasingly powerful uses of our data. The collection and management of data about individuals and groups has long been a central component of insurance practice. As historian Dan Bouk has shown, insurers have relied for over a century on information about populations in order to determine who is considered an acceptable risk, how much insurance to sell them, and at what price. Life insurers led the charge in this process, drawing on historical group, class, and racial characteristics, as well as medical information and mortality data, to manage and price policies held by hundreds of thousands of Americans before the turn of the twentieth century.

As is often the case in insurance history, other fields in the industry followed the lead of the life insurance sector. Property and casualty insurers followed life insurers in seeking out more refined classification structures—and in turning to public service initiatives as tools for gathering data and shaping consumer behavior. These companies used information collected in postwar driver education classes, for example, to set rates and sell policies. The Aetna Casualty and Surety Company's Drivotrainer course, designed in the 1950s, represented a particularly successful effort to systemize and quantify driving while also offering a means of gathering data on driver behavior. Indeed, the Drivotrainer simulator served as an early model for the development of telematic devices, which became popular data collection tools for the auto insurance industry in the early 2000s.

These devices, installed voluntarily in the vehicles of insurance consumers, gather data about braking behavior, driving speed, mileage, distance driven, and the time of day when a vehicle is in use. Premium discounts for consumers who install such devices have helped boost their popularity, despite concerns surrounding privacy—and the fact that insurers admit to selling recorded data to third parties. Like wearable fitness trackers and wellness apps, telematic devices are widely advertised by the insurance industry as evidence that insurance rate setting is fair and based on an individual's ability to responsibly manage their own risks.

Not all data used by insurers to price and classify risk is based on behavior individuals can easily control, however. For decades most insurance companies have based underwriting on broad group characteristics such as sex, age, and geographical location. By the 1960s, property and casualty insurers had developed rating structures that priced policies differently for older women and younger men, urban and suburban residents, divorcees, widows, unmarried cohabitating couples, and married couples with and without children. Today insurers continue to seek out new data sets and ever more refined classification schemes on which to base underwriting decisions. Credit scores are widely used to price auto and home insurance, for example: companies regularly charge consumers with low credit scores two, three, or even four times as much for coverage than consumers with higher credit scores and "equal risk." Though consumer advocates argue that credit-based insurance rating is unfair because such data has little relation to the risks associated with driving or homeownership, the industry has successfully evaded regulation of the practice in all but a handful of states.

Technological change and a growing willingness on the part of Americans to surrender personal data are also reshaping insurance practice. Life insurers began drawing on data gathered through wearable fitness trackers such as Apple watches and Fitbits in the early 2010s. Though insurance-based use of these devices began on a voluntary basis, some life and health insurers have recently moved to make fitness trackers compulsory for policyholders. The life insurance giant John Hancock, for example, made waves in 2018 when it announced that future consumers will be required to purchase "interactive policies" that include use of fitness trackers and wellness apps designed to ensure that policyholders actively maintain healthy lifestyles.

The potential for discrimination and abuse of data collected by fitness trackers is stark. In 2018 the state of West Virginia announced plans to revise its public workers health program, requiring all employees to use a fitness tracking app or pay an annual $500 fee. A historic nine-day strike launched by the state's teachers' union, which opposed the new health plan, scuttled the program. Without further resistance, however, others like it will no doubt become widespread in coming years. In 2019 Fitbit announced a new product: a wearable tracking device, Inspire, that will be made available to participating corporate employees and health insurance plan members. For workers employed by companies that adopt Fitbit-based health plans, the use of such devices will not likely be voluntary.

Attempts to regulate risk classification and data collection have achieved only limited success over the past fifty years, but resistance to these practices is growing. The increased availability of genomic data has set off warning bells that insurance companies may use genetic testing to discriminate against individuals with genetic risk indicators. As insurance law scholar Tom Baker notes, "While some 'low risk' individuals may believe that they are benefited by risk classification, any particular individual is only one technological innovation away from losing his or her privileged status."

Such fears spurred the 2008 Genetic Information Nondiscrimination Act (GINA), which forbids health insurers from using genetic information for risk classification and pricing. But the limitations of the bill are striking. It does not apply to those who receive health insurance through military service, the Veterans Health Administration, or the Indian Health Service. It does not protect against genetic discrimination in life, disability, or long-term care insurance. And it exempts "employee wellness" programs—a loophole that allows employers to use genetic tests to identify employee health risks and charge those who refuse testing hundreds or thousands of dollars more per year for coverage.

Will attempts to combat discriminatory use of data meet the same fate as earlier attempts by civil rights and feminist activists to abolish risk classifications based on sex and place of residence? Political will is often identified as a crucial factor in advancing regulation, but the success or failure of future battles with the industry will depend on more than the willingness of regulators to act. To attract widespread public support for change, insurance critics will need to challenge industry justifications for surveillance and risk classification that have circulated for decades. Understanding the complex historical contexts in which these practices developed—and the various strategies insurers have used to defend them—will prove valuable in coming fights with the industry.

BY THE MID-1990s, sociologists of risk and insurance had identified a large-scale shift in Western capitalist societies, away from compensatory "insurantial logics" and toward the "embrace of risk." This argument, popularized by Baker and sociologist Jonathan Simon in their 2002 book *Embracing Risk*, emphasized the celebration of risk-taking, particularly among elites, that became prevalent in the United States and other nations during the 1980s and 1990s.

Baker and Simon's work remains relevant today, but it largely overlooks the negative impacts of the privatization of risk. To speak of "embracing risk" suggests a choice, but many Americans have never had one. Forced to seek security via the private market, they were exposed to its whims. It was precisely the risk-taking behavior of financial elites that caused the Great Recession, and a privatized security system designed to shift the burden of risk onto individuals and away from corporations and government—a process political scientist Jacob Hacker calls the "Great Risk Shift"—only deepened the consequences of the economic crisis. The result has harmed most middle- and working-class Americans, who have been forced to take on the heavy burden of achieving security on their own, distanced and divorced from the collectives that might have offered a base to stand on.

The situation is not all bleak, however. Increasing precarity and exposure to risk have led to resistance, particularly among younger Americans. Calls to further regulate the insurance industry and politicize risk classification, to remove profit from the pursuit of security, and to build and expand public insurance programs have greatly multiplied since the financial crisis, and health insurance has emerged as a major site of activism and policy discussions in recent elections. This activism differs from earlier efforts in its willingness to directly challenge the profit motives of insurance companies, and, crucially, in its calls to abolish private health insurance as an industry. Nationalization of health insurance in the United States may very well lead to calls for expansion of other public insurance programs and the nationalization, or significant reform, of other insurance fields.

How might we build on this momentum to bring about a new insurance era? The first step will be understanding the basic workings of insurance and the often hidden role it plays in our lives. Insurance has long served as a reminder of the pervasiveness of uncertainty and our helplessness in the face of chance. But it also emboldens us as agents with the power to care for one another and to compensate for misfortune through

THE LIMITS OF SOCIAL SCIENCE
Lily Hu

IN 2016 economist Roland G. Fryer, Jr., the youngest African American ever to be awarded tenure at Harvard University, came upon what he would call the "most surprising result of my career." In a study of racial differences in the use of force by police officers, Fryer found that Black and Hispanic civilians were no more likely than white civilians to be shot to death by police. "You know, protesting is not my thing," Fryer told the *New York Times*. "But data is my thing. So I decided that I was going to collect a bunch of data and try to understand what really is going on when it comes to racial differences in police use of force."

Three thousand hours later, after meticulous records collection and analysis, the data had spoken. Although Black people are significantly more likely to experience *non-lethal* force at the hands of police than white people in similar situations, Fryer concluded, there is no racial bias in fatal police shootings. The findings appeared to have direct implications for the growing protest movement that had swept across the United States following the police killings of Michael Brown, Eric Garner, Tamir Rice, Freddie Gray, and Philando Castile, among so many others. "It is plausible that racial differences in lower-level uses of force," Fryer wrote at the end of the paper, "are simply a distraction and movements such as Black Lives Matter should seek solutions within their own communities rather than changing the behaviors of police and other external forces."

The study quickly came under fire. For the most part, critics took one of two tacks. One was to argue that the research failed on its own technical terms: the data were erroneous or misleading; there was a mathematical error in the analysis; the statistical protocol was inappropriate. The other tack was to undermine the legitimacy of the effort on auxiliary grounds, pointing out that economists are not experts in the study of police shootings and that the profession of economics suffers from a conservative bias. These two types of replies exemplify a common pattern of response to the results of quantitative social science, and they are also once again on wide display in national conversations about policing. But they illustrate a deep problem with the way we think about the nature of social scientific inquiry—and, consequently, its capacity to inform our thinking about politics and policy.

On these two views, scientific method is either so airtight that only errors from within can undermine it or so porous that its validity turns entirely on outside interests. There are certainly cases of each kind of blunder: recall the Reinhart-Rogoff Excel spreadsheet debacle on the one hand, tens of millions of dollars funneled by ExxonMobil to fund climate change denialism studies on the other.

We misunderstand run-of-the-mill scientific practice, however, if we view it as either everywhere or nowhere settled by data. As historians and philosophers of science have long emphasized, "the data" can never take us all the way from observation to conclusion; we can interpret them only against some background theory that settles what the data are evidence of. Far from playing no role in quantitative social science, a shared set of theoretical and normative commitments is what allows data-first methods to work at all.

This entwining of data and theory runs through any application of quantitative methods, but it is especially fraught today in the study of race. Since the 1970s, the development of causal inference methodology and the rise of large-scale data collection efforts have generated a vast quantitative literature on the effects of race in society. But for all its ever-growing technical sophistication, scholars have yet to come to consensus on basic matters regarding the proper conceptualization and measurement of these effects. What exactly does it mean for race to act as a cause? When do inferences about race make the leap from mere correlation to causation? Where do we draw the line between assumptions about the social world that are needed to get the statistical machinery up and running and assumptions that massively distort how the social world in fact is and works? And what is it that makes quantitative analysis a reliable resource for law and policy-making?

In both academic and policy discourse, these questions tend to be crowded out by increasingly esoteric technical work. But they raise deep concerns that no amount of sophisticated statistical practice can resolve, and that will indeed only grow more significant as "evidence-based" debates about race and policing reach new levels of controversy in the United States. We need a more refined appreciation of what social science can offer as a well of inquiry, evidence, and knowledge, and what it can't. In the tides of latest findings, what we should believe—and what we should give up believing—can never be decided simply by brute appeals to data, cordoned off from judgments of reliability and significance. A commitment to getting the social world right does not require deference to results simply because the approved statistical machinery has been cranked. Indeed in some cases, it may even require that we reject findings, no matter the prestige or sophistication of the social scientific apparatus on which they are built.

AN OBJECT LESSON in these issues can be found in a controversy ignited last summer when a paper published in the *American Political Science Review* (*APSR*) in late May questioned the validity of many recent approaches to studying racial bias in police behavior, including Fryer's. A very public skirmish among social scientists ensued, all against the backdrop of worldwide protests over the murder of George Floyd by Minneapolis police officer Derek Chauvin.

The *APSR* paper focused, in particular, on the difficulties of "studying racial discrimination using records that are themselves the product of racial discrimination." The authors—Dean Knox, Will Lowe, and Jonathan Mummolo—argued:

When there is any racial discrimination in the decision to detain civilians—a decision that determines which encounters appear in police administrative data at all—then estimates of the effect of civilian race on subsequent police behavior are biased absent additional data and/or strong and untestable assumptions.

The trouble, in short, is that "police records do not contain a representative sample" of people observed by the police. If there is racial bias reflected in who gets stopped and why—and we have independent reason to believe that it does—then police data for white and nonwhite arrestees are not straightforwardly comparable without making additional implausible or untestable assumptions. Such "post-treatment bias" in the data would thus severely compromise any effort to estimate the "true" causal effects of race on law enforcement behavior, even if we are only interested in what happens after the stop takes place. "Existing empirical work in this area is producing a misleading portrait of evidence as to the severity of racial bias in police behavior," the authors conclude. Such techniques "dramatically underestimate or conceal entirely the differential police violence faced by civilians of color." The authors therefore call for "future research to be designed with this issue in mind," and they outline an alternative approach.

A critical response by several other scholars—Johann Gaebler, William Cai, Guillaume Basse, Ravi Shroff, Sharad Goel, and Jennifer Hill—appeared a month later; for simplicity, call this group of scholars the *second camp*. Disputing the *APSR* authors' pessimistic assessment of research on racial bias in policing, they countered that the *APSR* paper rested on a "mathematical error." The usual methods *could* still recover reliable estimates of the causal effect of race on law enforcement behavior after a stop has been made, even if police stops are themselves racially biased. The error, they assert, lay in assuming that certain conditions *had* to be assumed in order to make reliable estimates using data like Fryer's. In fact, these scholars wrote, a weaker statistical condition—what they term "subset ignorability"—would also suffice, and it was more likely to hold, "exactly or approximately," in practice. They then attempted to show how the standard causal estimation techniques can be saved by putting forth their own analysis of racial bias in prosecutors' decisions to pursue charges (again relying on the sort of data from police records that the *APSR* authors find problematic).

In the days following this exchange, what ensued can only be described as a high-profile statistical showdown on Twitter, punctuated by takes from interested onlookers. The second camp mounted a defense of the mathematics, arguing that progress in statistical methods should not be foreclosed for fear of unobservable bias. In a policy environment that increasingly looks to quantitative analyses for guidance, Goel wrote, "categorically barring a methodology . . . can have serious consequences on the road to reform." The *APSR* authors, by contrast, emphasized what they took to be the purpose of applied social scientific research: to provide analysis at the service of real-world policy and practical political projects. Knox, for example, wrote that their critics' argument "treats racial bias like a game with numbers." Instead, he went on, he and his coauthors "use statistics to seek the best answers to serious questions—not to construct silly logic puzzles about knife-edge scenarios." This is no time, the *APSR* authors argued, to fetishize mathematical assumptions for the sake of cranking the statistical machinery.

WHAT ARE WE TO MAKE of this debate? Despite the references to mathematics and the sparring of proof, counterexample, disproof, which suggest a resolution is to be found only in the realm of pure logic, the dispute ultimately comes down to a banal, congenital feature of statistical practice: the plausibility of the assumptions one must make at the start of every such exercise. For the *APSR* authors, even the second camp's weaker assumption of subset ignorability fails the test of empirical scrutiny: to them it is clearly implausible as a matter of how the social world in fact is and works. Ironically though, given their forceful criticism of the *APSR* paper, the second camp comes to the same conclusion in their own analysis of prosecutors' charging decisions, conceding that "subset ignorability is likely violated"—thus rendering their own results empirically suspect.

This curious episode demonstrates how the social scientist is so often trapped in a double bind in her quest to cleave to her empirical commitments, especially when it comes to the observational studies— as opposed to randomized experiments—that are the bread and butter of almost all quantitative social science today. Either she buys herself the ability to work with troves of data, at the cost of implausibility in her models and assumptions, or she starts with assumptions that are empirically plausible but is left with little data to do inference on. By and large, quantitative social science in the last two decades has taken the former route, thanks in significant part to pressure from funding incentives. If implausible assumptions are the price of entry, the Big Data revolution promises the payment is worth it—be it in profit or professional prestige. As mathematical statistician David A. Freedman wrote, "In the social and behavioral sciences, far-reaching claims are often made for the superiority of advanced quantitative methods—by those who manage to ignore the far-reaching assumptions behind the models."

But if the social scientist is genuinely committed to being empirical, this choice she must make between plausible assumptions and readily available data must itself be justified on the basis of empirical evidence. The move she winds up making thus tacitly reveals the credence she has toward the theories of the social world presently available to her, or at least the kind of commitments she is willing to be wrong about. Precisely to the extent that social science is something more than mathematics —in the business of figuring out how the world is, or approximately is—statistical assumptions can never shake off their substantive implications. The requirement that social science be truly "evidence-based" is thus extremely demanding: it means that we cannot justify our use of implausible assumptions solely on the basis of mathematical convenience, or out of sheer desire to crank the statistical machinery. It is only in the belief that our assumptions are true, or true enough, of the actually existing world that social science can meet this exacting demand.

Notice the role that normativity plays in this analysis. If, as the first step to embarking on any statistical analysis, the quantitative social scientist must adopt a set of assumptions about how the social world works, she introduces substantive theoretical commitments as *inputs* into her inquiry. This initial dose of normativity thus runs through the entire analysis: there is simply no escaping it. Whether any subsequent statistical move is apt will depend, in however complex ways, on one's initial substantive views about the social world.

What do these reflections mean in the specific case of research on race and policing? Whether one has in fact distilled the causal effect of race on police behavior in any particular study will depend on what one believes to be true about the racial features of policing more broadly. And since what positions you take on these matters depend on your background views regarding the prevalence and severity of racial injustice as an empirical phenomenon, whether a finding ends up passing statistical muster and therefore counts as an instance of racially discriminatory police action will depend on your broader orientation to the social world.

The upshot of these considerations is that statistical analysis is inescapably norm-laden; "following the data" is never a mechanical or purely mathematical exercise. But this fact should not lead us to discard any commitment to empirical validity as such. On the contrary, it should simply serve to remind us that standards of empirical scrutiny apply throughout the whole of any methodology. As Freedman put it, "The goal of empirical research is—or should be—to increase our understanding of the phenomena, rather than displaying our mastery of technique."

ONE IMPORTANT CONSEQUENCE of this orientation, I think, is that we ought to subject not just assumptions but also conclusions to empirical scrutiny. To some observers of our social world, the conclusion that there is no causal effect of race in police shootings is not only implausible: it is simply and patently false. For even a cursory glance at descriptive summary statistics reveals wide gulfs in the risk of being killed by police for Blacks compared to whites. According to one study, Black men are about 2.5 times more likely to be killed by police than white men, and data from the 100 largest city police departments show that police officers killed unarmed Black persons at four times the rate of unarmed white persons—statistical facts that speak nothing of the immense historical record of overtly racist policing, which does not lend itself so easily to quantification. If certain methods erase these stark (and undisputed) disparities, painting a picture of a social landscape in which race does not causally influence police shooting behaviors, then so much worse for those methods. From this vantage, failing to take account of the many different forms of evidence of decades of racialized policing and policymaking is not only normatively wrong. It is also empirically absurd, especially as a self-styled "evidence-based" program that seeks to illuminate the truths of our social world.

This suggestion—that we sometimes ought to reject a finding on the grounds that it does not accord with our prior beliefs—might seem downright heretical to the project of empirical science. And indeed, there is some danger here; at the extreme, indiscriminate refusal to change our minds in the light of evidence reeks of a sham commitment to empirical study of the world. But the truth is that scientists reject findings on these sorts of grounds *all the time* in the course of utterly routine scientific practice. (For just one recent newsworthy example, consider a 2011 study that found evidence for extrasensory perception.) The move need not signal a failure of rationality; indeed it can often be a *demand* of it. Determining which it is, in any particular case, cannot be settled by asking whether one has been faithful to "facts and logic," as so many like to say, or to the pure rigors of mathematical deduction.

Instead, when a scientific finding conflicts with one of our convictions, each of us must comb over what philosopher W. V. O. Quine so charmingly called our "web of belief," considering what must be sacrificed so that other beliefs might be saved. And since our webs are not all identical, what rational belief revision demands of us will also vary. One man's happily drawn conclusion (*p*, therefore *q*!) is another's proof by contradiction (surely not *q*, therefore not *p*!). Or as the saying goes, one man's *modus ponens* is another man's *modus tollens*. Rejecting a study's methods or its starting assumptions on the basis of disagreement with its results is a completely legitimate inferential move. We tend to overlook this feature of science only because for most of us, so much of the nitty-gritties of scientific inquiry have little direct bearing on our daily lives. Our webs of belief usually are not touched by the latest developments in science. But once scientific findings make contact with—and perhaps even run up against—our convictions, we become much more sensitive to the way the chain of reasoning is made to run.

The fact that good faith efforts at rationality might lead different people to different or even opposite conclusions is a basic, if unsettling, limitation of science. We cannot hope for pure knowledge of the world, deductively chased from data to conclusion without mediating theory. In the end, the Fryer study controversy has been one long object lesson in how our empirical commitments are invariably entangled with normative ones, including commitments more typically thought of as ethical or political. The choice to sacrifice empirical plausibility in one's assumptions, in particular, is not just a "scientific" matter, in the oversimplified sense of "just the facts": it is inevitably interwoven with our ethical and political commitments. In bringing one's web of beliefs to bear on the debate over what constitutes proper study of effects of race in policing, one puts forth not just prior empirical beliefs about, say, the prevalence of racial targeting or the fidelity of police reporting practices, but also one's orientation toward matters of racial justice and self-conceptualization as a researcher of race and the broader system of policing and criminal justice.

For the *APSR* authors, bias in policing presents both enough of a normative concern and an empirical possibility to license, as a matter of good scientific practice, the sacrifice of certain business-as-usual approaches. The second camp, by contrast, is loath to make the leap to discard approaches held in such high esteem. Their commitment to the usefulness of the standard approaches runs so deep that they do not yet see sufficient cause for retreat. In a revision of their paper released in October, the authors remove the explicit assertion of a "mathematical error" but find "reason to be optimistic" that many cases of potential discrimination *do* meet the empirical conditions prescribed by the statistical assumptions proposed to salvage the usual approaches.

What exactly these reasons for optimism are remains unclear. By the second camp's own admission, because "one cannot know the exact nature and impact of unmeasured confounding . . . we must rely in large part on domain expertise and intuition to form reasonable conclusions." And yet without reference to any such further evidence or support, they nevertheless conclude: "In this case, we interpret our results as providing moderately robust evidence that perceived gender and race have limited effects on prosecutorial charging decisions in the jurisdiction we consider." Such a claim ultimately says much more about their web of belief than about the actually existing social world.

FOR THOSE WHOSE BELIEFS, empirical and ethical, are forged in participation in radical sociopolitical movements from below, to be ill-inclined to accept certain findings about race and policing is to remain steadfast in a commitment to a certain thick set of empirical and ethical propositions in *their* webs of beliefs: that systems of policing and prisons are instruments of racial terror and that any theory of causation, theory of race, and statistical methods worth their salt will see race to be a significant causal factor affecting disparate policing and prison outcomes. *This* just is the first test of "fitting the data." It is not a flight from rationality but an exercise of it.

Does this view of social science transform an epistemic enterprise into a crudely political one? Does a readiness to sacrifice some scientific findings to save ethical or political commitments endanger the status of science as a distinctive project that seeks to produce new knowledge about the world? I think it doesn't have to. Even the hardest-nosed empiricist starts from somewhere. She must interpret her data against some background theory that she takes to be the most natural, most plausible, and most fruitful. Deviations from this position that are self-consciously animated by politics need not be less genuinely truth-seeking than self-styled neutral deference to the status quo.

This fact tends to get lost in debates about where science sits along a continuum that runs from "objective" (protected from bias and outside interference) to "political" (a no-holds-barred struggle for power, the label of "science" slapped onto whatever the winner wishes). What that picture elides is how science unfolds in the trenches of knowledge production: in the methodological minutiae that determine which assumptions must be sacrificed and which can be saved, when abstraction leads to silly logic puzzles and when it is a necessary evil, which conclusions trigger double-takes and which signal paradigm shifts, and so on. To acknowledge that these struggles cannot take us beyond the never-ending tides of the "latest findings" is not to give up on quantitative social science as a venture for better understanding the world. It is simply to embrace a conception of social inquiry that is always, as philosopher Richard J. Bernstein put it, at once "empirical, interpretative, and critical."

SEEKING CERTAINTY IN UNCERTAIN TIMES
Michael Jackson

IN THE FACE of catastrophic climate change, I am surely not alone in wondering what point there is in writing about phenomena that render thought, action, and language seemingly so futile. Yet, as an anthropologist who has lived and worked in New Zealand, Australia, Sierra Leone, Denmark, and the United States, I have spent many years exploring the practical, ritual, and conceptual ways that people create hope in even the most hopeless situations.

Experience has taught me that the loss and recovery of a sense of certainty, like the loss and recovery of faith or wellness, is sometimes enabled by scientific knowledge, sometimes by magical thinking, and that human beings typically and opportunistically switch between these alternative survival strategies. Despite knowing that we will die, we create myths of invincible heroes, beliefs in reincarnation, concepts of an afterlife, and philosophies based on incontrovertible truth. Or we split body from mind, construing the former mortal and the latter immortal.

Moreover, when we recount our life stories in terms of a progression from confusion to clarity or the realization of childhood dreams, are we not conjuring the same illusion of certainty and order that we create in our homes and workplaces by establishing everyday routines, or that the scholar produces in a well-argued essay? These activities may, of course, be vindicated on practical grounds. An untidy house is unhygienic, a person without a plan in life will not succeed, an essay without a conclusion will not earn a passing grade. But these actions are ritualistic. They foster an illusion of certainty in an inherently chaotic world. Though they may be dismissed as magical, illusory, or irrational, they are existentially necessary for achieving the kind of provisional certainty without which our lives would be unlivable.

Consider storytelling. In Joan Didion's compelling phrase, "We tell ourselves stories in order to live." Stories are a means whereby we recount and rework events that simply befall us. We do this partly by sharing our experience with others in a form they can relate or respond to, thereby reaffirming and consolidating our sense of belonging to a family, a circle of friends, a community, or even a nation. But we also tell stories as a way of transforming our sense of who we are, recovering a sense of ourselves as actors and agents in the face of experiences that render us insignificant, unrecognized, or powerless. As David Grossman puts it, storytelling counters the arbitrariness of existence; it allows one the freedom "to articulate the tragedy of [one's] situation in [one's] *own words*." Writing affords us the same existential consolation, for "from the moment we take pen in hand or put fingers to keyboard, we have already ceased to be at the mercy of all that enslaved and constrained us before we began writing."

Existentially, storytelling and writing resemble occult technologies such a prayer, ritual sacrifice, divination, and dream interpretation. In the following account of beginning fieldwork in a remote Kuranko village in northern Sierra Leone many years ago, I invoke the precariousness of living outside one's cultural comfort zone as a way of exploring more general questions about how we cope with uncertainty.

NOT LONG AFTER ARRIVING in the village that would, in time, become my second home, I had a disturbing dream that I recorded immediately on waking. The dream comprised two episodes.

In the first episode of the dream, I found myself in a bare room, reminiscent of one of the classrooms at the Kabala District Council Primary School where I had first met Noah Marah, who was a teacher before taking leave to work as my field assistant. Through an open corrugated iron door, a book was passed into the room by an invisible hand or some other invisible agency. The book hung suspended in midair for several seconds and I identified a single word in bold type on its cover: ETHNOGRAPHY. I had the impression that the book contained only blank pages.

In the second episode, I found myself again in the same room. Again, the door opened. I felt a tremendous presence sweep into the room. I felt myself lifted up and, as if held in the hands of a giant, I was taken out of the room. The hands and arms of the giant exerted such pressure against my chest that I could not breathe easily. I was borne along aloft, still being squeezed. At this point I awoke in fear.

The dream clearly manifested several of my anxieties at that time: my uncertainty about carrying out my research for a thesis or book on the Kuranko; my dependence on Noah, who initially mediated all my relationships with Kuranko people and who was instructing me in the language; the mild paranoia, vulnerability, and alienation I experienced in the villages surrounded by people I did not know and talk I did not understand.

The day after this dream, Noah and I made a trip to a village, Dankawali, about twenty-five miles from my home base in Kabala. There I met the brother of Alpha Kargbo II, a Kuranko elder with whom I had spent some time in Kabala during the preceding weeks. On learning that Alpha's brother, Fode, was adept in dream interpretation, I recounted my dream to him. He was puzzled, and the dream was discussed among other elders. Some confusion arose from my reference to a giant, since the word could not be translated exactly into Kuranko. The nearest equivalent to our word giant is *ke yan* (literally, "long man"), designating a tall bush spirit that sometimes allies itself with a hunter. I was told that if this bush spirit appears in a dream, it wishes to help the dreamer. I was asked whether the giant flew up into the sky with me, and whether he had placed me back on the ground. After I had answered these questions, Fode announced the meaning of the dream: it signified importance, it meant that if I were a Kuranko man I would be destined to become a chief. Fode added, "You will become a very important person; I do not know about you because you are a European, but for us the book means knowledge; it came to reveal knowledge."

Despite Fode's caveat—that he might not be able to interpret a European's dream using Kuranko hermeneutics—his elucidation of the meaning of the dream was consistent with orthodox Kuranko readings. A book signifies knowledge; being in a strange place among strange people signifies good fortune in the near future; being in a high place signifies the imminent attainment of a prestigious position; flying like a bird signifies happiness and prosperity.

Where Fode's interpretation differed from my own wasn't only at the level of exegesis; it was in his conviction that the dream presaged future events rather than revealed present anxieties. Nevertheless, his assurances did help allay my anxieties, and I felt that his interpretation of my dream consisted in more than pat references to commonplace Kuranko images—a fish with scales foretelling the birth of a son, a fish without scales foretelling the birth of a daughter, being in a dark forest or a swamp signifying a conspiracy, and so forth. Fode's interpretation suggested conscious or unconscious sympathy for my situation as a stranger in his society.

My emotions during this transitional time were very mixed. Behind me was the Cambridge academic world in which I had been steeped, a world of ostensible order, both academic and architectural, and of scholarly routines and college protocols that dated back centuries. Before me lay a world of bewildering otherness, a language I strained to hear, lives I struggled to understand, tastes I could not get used to, beliefs I could not get my head around. There was also the anxiety of living apart from my wife for weeks on end, and the difficulties of reconciling my hope for friendship with Noah with the fact that he was my paid assistant.

After four weeks in the village of Firawa, and with no means of communicating with my wife Pauline in Kabala, I had become increasingly concerned for her well-being. Although Noah's wives had promised to keep Pauline company and help her with marketing, and she was busy with her dissertation research on the Icelandic family sagas, I was worried that in the event of a medical emergency, her life and the life of the child she was carrying might be in danger.

My anxieties came to a head one evening when I went out to the latrine that stood in the grassland behind the house where I was staying. The silence was suddenly broken by several Senegal firefinches flitting around me. Aware that for Kuranko these small crimson birds embody the souls of children who have died in infancy, I became convinced that Pauline had had a miscarriage and that her life was in peril.

That night I slept fitfully, and in the morning confided my fears to Noah. He too was missing his children and wondering about his wives; perhaps it was time for us to return to Kabala.

That afternoon, Noah announced that he was going to see a diviner, Bockari Wularé, and invited me to accompany him.

A diviner is "one who lays out pebbles" (*beresigile*) or reads palms (*bolomafelne*, literally "hand-on-looker"), though other divinatory techniques include mirror-reading and consulting the Qu'ran. Bockari used river stones.

We were taken indoors, and sat on either side of a raffia mat spread on the clay floor.

After observing Bockari divine for Noah, I asked if he could read the stones for me.

I half expected Bockari to scoff at my request, but he responded without a word, and began following the same procedure he had followed with Noah.

"Why have you come?" he asked.

Noah spoke for me. "He wants to find out about his wife. She is expecting a child. He is worried about her. He wants to know if all is well, and if all will be well."

Bockari emptied some stones from his small monkey-skin bag and with the palm of his hand spread them across the mat. Most were river pebbles: semitranslucent, the color of rust, jasper, and yellow ocher. Among them were some cowrie shells, old coins, and pieces of metal. When I handed Bockari his fifty-cent consultation fee, he mingled it with these objects.

"What is your wife's name?"

"Pauline," I answered, pleased to have understood the question.

Bockari found difficulty with the name but did not ask for it to be repeated. In a soft voice he addressed the stones, informing them of the reason I had come. Then he gathered up a handful and began to chant. At the same time, with half-closed eyes, he rhythmically knocked the back of his cupped hand against the mat.

Very deliberately, he then laid out the stones, some in pairs, some singly, others in threes and fours.

"All is well," Bockari said quietly, his attention fixed on the stones. "Your wife is well. She will give birth to a baby girl."

Without pausing, he proceeded to lay out a second pattern.

"There is nothing untoward. The paths are clear. The birth will be easy."

To see what sacrifice I should make, Bockari laid out the stones a third time.

"Your wife must sacrifice some clothes and give them to a woman she respects. You must sacrifice two yards of white satin and give it to a man you respect. When your child is born, you must sacrifice a sheep."

Bockari looked warily at me, as if wondering whether I would do what the stones demanded.

"To whom must I address the sacrifice of the sheep?" I asked in English. Noah translated.

"To your ancestors," Bockari said.

Though reassured by Bockari's insights, I could not resist pressing him to explain how he arrived at them.

"How can the stones tell you what to tell me?" I asked, again relying on Noah to translate.

"They speak, just as we are speaking now. But only I can hear what they are saying. It is a gift that I was born with."

"Could I acquire that gift?"

"A person cannot tell if a bird has an egg in its nest simply by watching it in flight."

I told Noah that I did not understand.

Bockari fetched the loose sleeve of his gown up onto his shoulder and frowned. "You cannot go looking for it. It comes to you."

There was a silence.

"Come, let's eat," Bockari said, climbing to his feet. He stowed his bag of stones between a rafter and the thatch, then wrenched the raffia door open. The sunlight blinded me.

When we were seated in the yard, we took it in turns to wash our hands before Bockari's wife brought us an enamel dish, piled high with rice and peanut sauce.

"How did you get the stones?" I asked. "And the words you say to them—did someone teach them to you?"

Bockari finished his mouthful of rice. Then, as if amused by my curiosity, he said cryptically, "If you find fruit on the ground, look to the tree."

I must have looked perplexed but Bockari continued. "I began divining a long time ago, in the days of Chief Pore Bolo. I was favored by a djinn. I saw a djinn, and the djinn told me it was going to give me some stones so that I would be able to help people."

"Where did you see the djinn?"

"In a dream. They came in a dream. There were two of them. A man and a woman. They had changed themselves into human beings and were divining with river stones. They called to me and told me their names. They said, 'We are going to favor you with a different destiny.' They showed me a certain leaf and told me I should make it into a powder and mix it with water in a calabash. Then I was to get some stones from the river and wash them in that liquid. When I woke up the next morning I went to the river and found that leaf and those stones. I did everything the djinn told me to do."

"Would I be able to find that leaf?"

"Eh! I cannot tell you about that!"

"The djinn then, did you see them again?"

"Yes, I see them often. Every Thursday and Friday night they appear to me in a dream. Sometimes they say to me, 'Are you still here?'"

"Do the djinn speak to you through the stones?"

"Yes," Bockari said, as if pleased that I had finally understood something of what he was telling me.

"When you address the stones, you are speaking to the djinn?"

"No! I am speaking to the stones." A frown creased Bockari's forehead. Hitching up his sleeve, he scooped a ball of rice from the calabash and slipped it deftly into his mouth.

I had finished eating, but not my questioning. "Do you ever give anything to the djinn?"

Bockari swallowed the rice and washed it down with some water. "From time to time I offer them a sacrifice of white kola nuts."

I could see Bockari was tired, and that Noah was exasperated by my questions and the difficulty of translating them. I got up to go, and Noah followed.

Once we got back to Kabala, I shared my experience with Pauline, who was as reassured by Bockari's confident predictions as I had been, and I wasted no time in making the sacrifices I had been directed to make to ensure that the birth of our daughter went smoothly. I was curious, however, to find myself acting as if I had embraced the assumptions on which Kuranko divinatory praxis was based. Could this be compared to an agnostic turning to God at a critical crossroads in life, or an alcoholic admitting his or her powerlessness as a first step on the road to recovery? Was there a necessary relationship between belief and action, or were beliefs best seen as coping mechanisms whose efficacy was only arbitrarily connected to their epistemological status?

Five years would pass before I published my praxeological account of Kuranko divination ("An Approach to Kuranko Divination,"

Jackson

1978). Although I would refer in it to my consultation with Bockari, my findings reflected numerous conversations with diviners and their clients, and my conclusions would run counter to the prevailing epistemological approach to divination in anthropology. Influenced by the rationality–irrationality debate, many anthropologists asked how diviners were able to maintain credibility and protect the plausibility of a diagnostic system that was, at best, hit and miss.

By contrast, my focus was on the experiences of clients who did not know what to think or do when faced by a perilous journey, a difficult childbirth, a troubling dream, a grave illness, a sudden death, an impending initiation, or even building a new house and making a new farm. What appeared to be submission to a higher power was a prelude to regaining control over one's fate. Though the power attributed to djinn or diviners might be illusory, it entailed real effects, and insofar as it alleviated anxiety and restored a sense of agency and certainty, it did not necessarily inspire retrospective interest in the existence of djinn or the veracity or fallibility of the diviner's methods.

My interpretation was consonant with the pragmatist spirit of Kuranko thought. The critical issue was not whether a story told, a prognosis offered, or a sacrifice made met some abstract standard of rationality but whether it encouraged hope, bolstered one's spirits, and offered a new way of thinking about a recurrent dilemma. As philosopher William James put it in his book *Pragmatism* (1907), truth is what "*happens* to an idea. It *becomes* true, is *made* true by events. Its verity *is* in fact an event, a process."

WE ALL NEED a degree of certainty and predictability in our lives. My own experiences of Kuranko divination—whose prescribed actions helped alleviate my anxieties even though I did not subscribe to Kuranko "beliefs" in the supernatural agents that guided the divinatory process—convinced me that all humans need to feel that they can act and speak with some likelihood that their actions will draw a response from others and even change the world. But our words are often misconstrued, our intentions misinterpreted, and our very existence ignored. It is, to borrow Ralph Ellison's phrase, as if we are socially invisible and our lives do not matter. Such unresponsiveness can undermine our self-worth and degrade our humanity.

Such experiences are traumatic enough in the context of our lives with others, but what about when we are struck by the unresponsiveness of the extra-human world—the world of things, viruses, objects, oceans, landscapes, and ever-changing climatic conditions? For psychoanalytic anthropologist George Devereux, the unresponsiveness of the material world can be as traumatic as the unresponsiveness of other people—or, as several Holocaust memoirists record, the unresponsiveness of God in their hour of need. That the material and extra-human world is beyond our capacity to fully comprehend and control explains why, in Devereux's view, we endow the physical world with anthropomorphic characteristics. This strategy makes the entire universe appear to be subject to the same rules of reciprocity, recognition, and responsiveness that operate in the human realm. If we can make sacrifices or offerings to gods, persuading them to act benignly toward us, we act as if the extra-human world were not completely alien, but susceptible to the same bargaining we use in our everyday face-to-face relations with our fellow humans.

It is worth remembering, in this regard, that for small children, the boundary between their internal world and the physical world is fluid and often blurred. Self and external world are often experienced as all of a piece. This led Swiss child psychologist Jean Piaget to argue that the child's conception of the world is animistic; what to an adult seems inanimate is, for the child, often imbued with vitality. Children readily assume that inanimate things have consciousness and will. A kicked table will feel hurt, a moving bicycle knows where it is going, the sun looks at us with its rays. Only gradually does the child recognize the difference between human beings and the rest of the world. Thus, a nine-year-old, when asked, "Can a fire feel anything?" answers, "No," just as most adults would. "If someone threw water on the fire, would it feel that?" "No." "Why not?" "Because it is not a person."

Devereux extends Piaget's thesis by arguing that *anyone* is likely to perceive the world in this animistic way, no matter his or her age, when he or she feels overwhelmed or threatened by the physical world. Treating it as animate helps us magically bring it within the ambit of our consciousness and control and provides us with means of acting on it.

Devereux shares with philosopher John Dewey the view that science and religion are not fundamentally different in this regard. Both are existential strategies for making the material or physical world around us appear less unresponsive to our control. We thus transform the deep uncertainty we feel toward the world around us into a provisional certainty. If I pray, do my duty, recycle my trash, offer sacrifices, study well, exercise patience, avoid giving offense, then the world will respect my efforts in the same way that another reasonable human being would.

This kind of magical thinking only gets us so far, however; it cannot fundamentally alter the nature of the universe. In his book *The Quest for Certainty* (1925), Dewey notes that "when all is said and done, the fundamentally hazardous character of the world [is never] seriously modified, much less eliminated," and he cites the impact of World War I to make his point. As a more recent example, we might offer the COVID-19 pandemic, for which science has developed effective vaccines yet which, for many people, continues to inspire conspiracy theories and superstitious fears. Moreover, as Dewey observes in *Experience and Nature* (1925), those who regard science as synonymous with certainty resemble those who turn to superstition: "Our magical safeguard against the uncertain character of the world is to deny the existence of chance, to mumble universal and necessary law, the ubiquity of cause and effect, the uniformity of nature, universal progress, and the inherent rationality of the universe."

Many people would agree that our collective future on Earth is now so imperiled and uncertain that neither science, nor government, nor religion can offer the assurances of certainty that we have traditionally expected from them. Although we often accept and even cultivate indeterminacy (as in gambling, high-risk sports, and risky business ventures), there is a threshold of tolerance beyond which chance ceases to be a matter of gambles willingly taken and becomes oppressive and unbearable.

For a lot of people this threshold has been crossed, and I am reminded of Albert Einstein's response to Werner Heisenberg's uncertainty principle, which states that we can never know whether subatomic matter is wave-like or particulate since our methods of investigating the phenomenon partly determine its apparent nature. When Einstein declared against the new physics, writing, "Quantum mechanics is very impressive, but I am convinced that God does not play dice," he was in a sense admitting the same intolerance of the aleatory that in a West African village leads a person to seek consolation in the predictive and systematizing powers of a diviner—for in divination, as in science, we hope to reduce ambiguity and arrive at provisional certitudes which will offer us "something to go on," to renew faith, bolster hope, and guide action in a precarious world.

WHAT GOOD CAN DREAMING DO?

Annie Howard

FIFTY YEARS AGO Ursula K. Le Guin's *The Lathe of Heaven* entered a world witnessing the once-hopeful dreams of the sixties curdling into the nightmare of neoliberal capitalism. First published in 1971, the novel puts Le Guin's distinctively artful combination of psychological and sociological themes with dynamic science fiction storytelling on full display, imagining a world in which dreaming could quite literally effect massive social change, for good as well as for ill. In its own moment, this message carried a cutting critique of hippie political idealism: while John Lennon was busy the same year singing, "You may say I'm a dreamer / but I'm not the only one," the growing reality of fracturing left-wing movements unable to carry out mass social change was becoming more apparent by the day. Reread today in our own moment of accumulating crises, *The Lathe of Heaven* invites us to reflect on the necessary but slippery role of radical imagination in the arsenal of progressive social movements, rendering dreams both an essential source of hope and a potential site for wishful thinking or frightful authoritarian deformation.

The book's core premise is simple. George Orr, living in a nightmarish world of ecological collapse, mass starvation, and political violence eerily reminiscent of our own, discovers a unique talent: the ability to remake reality through the power of what he calls "effective dreaming." Wracked with guilt over his ability to transform his surroundings so dramatically (first discovered as a child, when he inadvertently killed his aunt), Orr attempts to contain this power though dream-suppressing medication, which catches the attention of medical authorities. Forced into mandatory sleep therapy, his oneirologist Dr. William Haber soon wields Orr's worldmaking abilities to create a better world—at least, as he imagines it—by way of hypnotic suggestion, an approach that leads to countless unanticipated side effects. The path to a better world, the novel suggests, is not so straightforward, even when it is paved with good intentions.

The central dilemma lies in how to interpret the instructions Dr. Haber gives to Orr. The *conscious* mind might make one thing of an injunction to end human conflict—as Haber instructs Orr to dream at one point—but the *unconscious* is never so simple. At rest, our brain takes imaginative leaps; it finds ways of recombining waking reality in unlikely or even impossible formations, finding plasticity and elasticity where the waking, rational mind so often misses it. Coaxed through Haber's powers of suggestion to deliver a better world, Orr's dreamscape instead bends and feints, finding ways to match the doctor's formal commands even as it creates a world he did not intend.

In this sense, *The Lathe of Heaven* meditates on Le Guin's Taoist principles. Le Guin, who also produced a translation of the *Tao Te Ching*, has Orr embody a noninterventionist perspective in the novel. He mainly feels disinterest toward his world-changing gift; his preference would be simply to never use it. When his efforts to suppress his dreaming prove unsuccessful, he opposes Haber's attempts to weaponize and instrumentalize his power.

Orr is wiser than Haber about how difficult it is to align conscious desire with the unconscious's uncertainty, and how this will invariably cause Haber's instructions to backfire. Orr's own imagination proves, again and again, incapable of conceiving of the hopeful outcomes he'd still like to see:

> You said, no killing of humans by other humans. So I dreamed up the Aliens. Your own ideas are sane and rational, but this is my unconscious you're trying to use, not my rational mind. . . . You're trying to reach progressive, humanitarian goals with a tool that isn't suited to the job. Who has humanitarian dreams?

As Orr suggests, imagination is at once a fount of incredible optimism *and* a stubborn realm in which latent fear and anxiety can manifest. Political philosopher Fredric Jameson's observation that "it has become easier to imagine the end of the world than the end of capitalism" crystallizes this dilemma: while the revolutionary project must claim the mantle of dreaming up better worlds to come, we are also fighting against the tide—not just figuratively but literally, in the face of ever more terrifying climate change.

Of course, Le Guin is not the only person who's been fascinated by the realm of the unconscious as a site for social and political exploration. Whether in the psychedelic politics of sixties guru

Timothy Leary, the magical realist-inflected Marxism of writer Andy Merrifield, or the similar effort made in cultural critic Mark Fisher's *Acid Communism* (unfinished at the time of his death in 2017), an effort to blend the surprising imaginaries of unconscious thought with rigorous political action has been a constant theme of the past half-century's utopian radicalisms. All of these divergent projects reveal similar tensions, namely a concern with solipsistic exploration and the need to plug individual insights about the unknown into a larger framework for social change. In that sense, *The Lathe of Heaven* is a natural touchstone in this conversation, modeling the messy challenges wrought by dabbling with unconscious forces beyond our control.

BEYOND THE SPECIFIC UNLOOSENING of reality that's carried out in sleep, *The Lathe of Heaven* is also a good reminder that our politics deserve a greater level of imagination, play, and creativity than we often afford them. Without making an end-run around the material conditions we face, as Dr. Haber attempts to do by wielding Orr's effective dreams with blunt force, there are nonetheless plenty of ways we can approach politics differently—if we are willing to enact a degree of chance or even chaos to unsettle the encrustation of a lifeless realism.

That's the main thrust of Merrifield's study *Magical Marxism: Subversive Politics and the Imagination* (2011). Merrifield reads Gabriel García Márquez's *One Hundred Years of Solitude* (1967) alongside philosopher Guy Debord's *Society of the Spectacle* (1967) to inject magical realism into an analysis of the image-saturated reality that Debord diagnosed four years before *The Lathe of Heaven* was published. As Merrifield suggests, it's not as if we cannot already begin to access different realities within our own "if we look hard enough; it's just a question of changing one's perception about what reality is, about what politics is, about what it can be, ought to be." But where contemporary Marxists are often content to revel in the dour "realism of critical negativity," sharpening a critique of a society whose failed state is no secret to anyone suffering through it today, Merrifield insists that Marxists can remain critically engaged while expanding their power to conjure unforeseen worlds.

This move is not new to Marxism. Karl Marx himself, on a poetic streak in *The Eighteenth Brumaire of Louis Bonaparte* (1852), argued that the movement should fight to create a "poetry of the future." Central to this struggle is a battle over our dreams, a realm haunted by our greatest fears of what may be and leavened by untold possibilities yet to be realized. Merrifield suggests that dreaming and magical realism are both capable of pushing us past a dry materialism: "Magical Realism has as its muse actual reality, yet converts this often stark reality into fantasy, into fantastic and phantasmal subjective visions that become more real than objective reality itself." Willfully giving up control over reality, as we do in dreaming, is not an easy proposition. Still, given the lack of a stable future in an era of climactic chaos, our ability to anticipate what comes next will be tested in ways that demand more room for unpredictability.

At its best, dreaming up new worlds is a collective process, an undertaking too vast for one person to handle alone. That's the vision of poet Renee Gladman and artist Edie Fake in their shape-shifting, otherworldly *Paris Review* piece "Cities of the Future, Their Color": with our old images of futuristic cities now "codified and photographed and renovated," their productive capacities to remake reality now spent, the *"cities of the future* came to everyone one night in our sleep," inviting new opportunities to reflect on remaking the worlds we inhabit. The future cities imagined by Gladman and Fake are an invitation to find hope in what might become, and to hold a thoughtful mirror to present-day short-comings. In dreaming up such unrealized cities, one has "to be speculative" while bearing in mind what is "actually happening on your streets, in your bodies, and between bodies," in a way that recalls the thread of imagination-in-collective-action that ran through the uprisings of summer 2020. While everyday re-ality often dampens the spirit of creation—makes it impossible to believe that positive change can be sustained—being in con-versation with the dreams of others is a path toward rekindling a radical movement brimming with joyful co-creation of heretofore unrealized realities.

The Lathe of Heaven does not allow us to consider how a collective dream process might unravel currently existing real-ity, as the world-remaking power of dreaming is rooted only in Orr's unconscious. But it does offer an explicit critique of Dr. Haber's solipsistic certainty that dictating Orr's dreams is the best vehicle for positive change. Le Guin makes Orr into a beatific, Taoist embodiment of noninterventionism, one who understands that meddling with powerful unconscious forces is an easy path toward self-destruction. Orr's first uncontrolled effective dream as an adult comes as he and everything around him stands at the brink of final collapse: with the country run as an authoritarian police state, the population thinned by multiple epidemics and mass starvation, Orr collapses at the edge of the city, certain he won't wake up the next day. While the reality he faces the next morning cannot erase many of the failures of what came before, Orr's unconscious is still capable of conjuring a world ever-so-slightly more livable than where he came from, itself a miracle that leads him to despair at the thought of changing conditions any further.

After suppressing dreaming for a time, Orr's imagination is wielded by Dr. Haber, to increasingly dire outcomes. Instructed to dream a less overcrowded world, Orr creates a plague which kills 6 billion people; encouraged to eliminate human conflict, Orr conjures an alien threat that unites humanity in a common cause. He eliminates racial differences by turning the entire population into a gray, undifferentiated whole, in the process disappearing Heather Lelache, a mixed-race woman with whom he is in love. Each iteration pushes the world further from where it needs to be, and Orr begs Dr. Haber to reconsider his rationalist approach:

> We're in the world, not against it. It doesn't work to try to stand outside things and run them, that way. It just doesn't work, it goes against life. There is a way but you have to follow it. The world is, no matter how we think it ought to be. You have to be with it. You have to let it be.

Howard

Orr's pleading is to no avail, and the book ends with the planet forever unsettled by the mixed realities enacted by too much meddling. Frustrated by Orr's continued resistance, Dr. Haber eventually trains his own brain to dream effectively, but loses his mind to the knowledge of countless overlapping worlds. Earth is thereafter layered with multiple timelines at once, with aliens now settled on the planet as an everyday presence.

In that sense, the final, jumbled world of *The Lathe of Heaven* enacts the Zapatista philosophy of building "a world where many worlds fit," with the eventual creation of a more enduring, if confusing, environment still better than the one that Orr first unconsciously sought to change. Yet the many conscious interventions made in between, all in the name of positive social progress, are ultimately a force for incredible harm. It's a challenging, unsettling proposition for those who might look to Le Guin for political guidance. Can we really let the world be when the entire future of our planet seems to hang in the balance? Such questions have only grown more dire in the half century since the book was written; even at its release, with the once-flowering hippie political movement wilting at an alarming rate, Le Guin seemingly understood how vital these questions were to the longevity of radical political movements.

LE GUIN'S NOVEL EMERGED at a moment—1971—when the reality principle of a stable and enduring capitalism had proven highly vulnerable. Loosened by a flood of LSD and other psychedelic drugs that remapped culture and politics in the late sixties, many suburban-bred white teenagers found themselves unmoored from their parent's Protestant work ethic and cultural conservatism, just as Black Power and decolonial movements haunted the forces of global capital. If their defection from what economist John Kenneth Galbraith called "the affluent society" could be made permanent, young white people were primed to play a vital sustaining role in deepening this state of revolt into lasting societal change, their perception of the possible expanded by chemicals that exposed the fundamental brittleness of what surrounded them.

In this tempest of sixties psychedelic radicalism, there was no one more willing to anoint himself with god-like (or at least prophet-like) powers than Timothy Leary. Charismatic, endlessly quotable, the Harvard researcher and psychonaut became the figurehead of psychedelic consciousness both within and outside the hippie subculture. To his believers, he was a heroic figure, pushing the boundaries of human consciousness at unprecedented speeds; to his foes, he was a wanted man, just as dangerous as the Black Panthers, particularly for his influence on white youths.

But Leary's vision was cloudy when it came to the enduring materiality of racial capitalism in the United States, a limitation that became clear while he was in exile in Algeria, camped out with a sect of Black Panthers who'd offered him refuge. In one sense, Leary's infamous mantra—"Turn on, tune in, drop out"—aligned him with the kind of Taoist noninterventionism encouraged in *The Lathe of Heaven*. But in reality, Leary's insistence on nonaction foundered on the growing backlash to the era's radical tempest, as he underestimated just how rooted the conservative beliefs ran within the U.S. unconscious, the kind of lingering communal belief system that makes a nightmare of even our most hopeful fantasies.

Even before he fled the United States, Leary had already argued against mass political action as the next step for the counterculture. In a debate published after the 1966 Love Pageant Rally in San Francisco, Leary pushed against poet Allen Ginsberg and Buddhist philosopher Gary Snyder, who exhorted the movement to become more engaged. By contrast, Leary preached inner change: "I think they should be sanctified, drop out, find their own center, turn on, and above all avoid mass movements, mass leadership, mass followers." Whatever path was chosen, the road ahead remained open in that moment, the large-scale gatherings of disaffected youth seeming to stand for radical transformation just around the corner.

The mood had soured just five years later: Richard Nixon was at the height of his powers, the Vietnam War raged on, and political repression had eroded much of the material gains of the Panthers and other radical formations. Despite that, Leary continued to insist on an individualized, drug-oriented form of oppositional consciousness. The limitations of this approach are strikingly revealed in a 1971 issue of underground paper *Berkeley Tribe*, in which Black Panther leader Eldridge Cleaver challenged Leary's vacuousness in an interview carried out in Algiers, where the Panthers shielded Leary and his wife in exile.

Cleaver is clear that psychedelics were vital to radicalizing young white people whose lives were otherwise a million miles away from the material deprivation faced by Black America. But if psychedelics cracked open reality for so many, it was only a first step, not itself capable of unmaking the solid stubbornness of racial capitalism. As he argued:

> We do recognize the progressive role played in the past by the whole youth, drug, culture in the United States. It was very useful some years ago when people rebelled against the straitjacket rules and regulations of Babylonian society by turning away from the standards and values of that society, and by shattering to smithereens those values by getting high, freaking out, freaking off. . . . But things have changed since then. . . . We want people to gather their wits, to sober up, and get down to the serious business of destroying the Babylonian empire.

Chiding Leary, Abbie Hoffman, Jerry Rubin, and other white leadership for leaving their constituency in limbo, Cleaver recognized how the absence of a reality principle capable of filling the void opened by psychedelic consciousness left these young people vulnerable to empty navel-gazing. Especially as other elements of white-led radical movements such as the Weather Underground opted for spectacular violence to disrupt U.S. society, the lack of a middle path between outward social engagement and inward emotional transformation proved a significant undoing for the era's mass social upheavals. Threading such large-scale change between these competing influences would be a daunting task for any era of political radicals, of course; the added instability unleashed by psychedelics proved even more challenging.

The lack of sustainable connective tissue between Leary's individualistic approach to social change and the wider political movements of the era cannot be undone. Fortunately, there are some today who understand the value of seeking inner transformation on the way toward broader social transformation, recognizing that people are inherently changed by the process of struggling for a better world. That perspective is well embodied in the work of Reverend angel Kyodo williams, a Black queer Zen Buddhist instructor based in the Bay Area. In her book *Radical Dharma: Talking Love, Race, and Liberation* (2016), coauthored with Lama Rod Owens and Jasmine Syedullah, williams seeks to define a more balanced approach. "Without inner change," she writes, "there can be no outer change; without collective change, no change matters." Kyodo's patient, socially minded Buddhism is an invitation to continue seeking social change even when it feels as if our own actions can accomplish nothing. It is a method of guiding and shaping change without imposing our will, as Dr. Haber tries to do.

Difficult as it may be, there are still ways of threading these radical alternative political models into the existing organizing work carried out today. A clear counterpoint to Merrifield's Magical Marxism and Williams's Black, queer Buddhism is *Acid Communism*, the unfinished last book of influential Marxist cultural theorist Mark Fisher. As his title suggests, Fisher was seeking a through line in the many potentials unearthed by sixties counterculture, finding within various social, cultural, and political formations of the era a model of abundance that challenged capitalism's endless artificial scarcity.

Fisher proposes that a primary task of neoliberalism has been imposing what he calls "capitalist realism," or the false certainty that alternatives to our current economic model are "unthinkable." Memory of the sixties terrifies those who wish to maintain this repression, Fisher explains: "the decade haunts not because of some unrecoverable and unrepeatable confluence of factors, but because the potentials it materialized and began to democratize—the prospect of a life freed from drudgery—has to be continually suppressed." Fisher's interest in acid was less focused on its effects on individual consciousness and more on its widespread impacts on working-class culture, creating a sensibility that principles of free cultural expression and effective communal organization could be found. In the decades of neoliberalism that followed, Fisher suggests that "the failure of the left . . . had much to do with its repudiation of, or refusal to engage with, the dreamings that the counterculture unleashed." Unable to build a solid foundation on the shifting sands of a psychedelic culture that lacked deep roots in U.S. culture, and absent the kind of patient orientation to change that both Williams's Buddhism and Le Guin's Taoism encourage, we are instead left to remember this era with fading clarity.

IS THERE STILL TIME left for us to dream? A silly question, perhaps. And yet: everything about our politics today—from the looming danger of fascist violence to the seemingly inevitable destruction wrought by climate change—seems to necessitate an urgent response that pushes against our ability to slow down, let our minds wander, and simply conjure other worlds yet to be made. When crisis after crisis is not addressed, and the mere act of surviving each day is its own nightmarish struggle, allowing ourselves to dream can feel self-indulgent, trivial, the kind of luxury we deserve but are rarely afforded.

And yet dreams come to even the most run-down, burnt-out, flat-out-exhausted human being. What does it suggest about humanity that, however much we are subjugated, other worlds are always at hand in the quiet of night? In interviews, Le Guin pointed to other works, particularly the anarchist space colonies of her 1974 novel *The Dispossessed*, as her most political. But what if we held *The Lathe of Heaven* in that same space, considering what it means for how we think about politics? If nothing else, *The Lathe of Heaven* suggests that our dreams are best hashed out with others—that our individualistic fantasies, however expansive, are best actualized when meshed in conversation and collaboration, rather than cloistered in the narrow-minded pursuit of a single tendency or practice.

Recognizing the multiplicity of dreams that must be actualized is already at the core of many radical practices, as the Zapatista "world where many worlds fit" philosophy would suggest. Far more challenging is the act of moving in dialectical fashion from a dream state to waking existence, synthesizing a mixture of the two that neither delimits our imagination nor erases the hard work yet to be done of materially changing our surroundings. After a half century of being told that the radical demand for a transformed social and economic order was nothing more than a series of empty illusions, the choice to keep dreaming, even as we plant both feet firmly on the ground and in the streets, is exactly the kind of radical practice Le Guin would be proud of. As she suggested just a year after *The Lathe of Heaven* in her novella "The Word for the World is Forest" (1972): "Once you have learned to do your dreaming wide awake, to balance your sanity not on the razor's edge of reason but on the double support, the fine balance, of reason and dream; once you have learned that, you cannot unlearn it any more than you can unlearn to think."

WE DON'T KNOW, BUT LET'S TRY IT

Simon Torracinta

THIS SPRING THE UNITED STATES embarked on a grand experiment. The American Rescue Plan, signed into law on March 11, appropriated $1.9 trillion in public spending—on top of $2.2 trillion for the CARES Act a year prior—to accelerate recovery from the dramatic economic shock of the pandemic. Combined, these measures amount to a fiscal stimulus of unprecedented scale.

Economists in the Biden administration and the Federal Reserve are bullish that this intervention will enable a rapid return to the boom times—or at least what passed for them—that preceded March 2020. They believe that running the economy "hot," without much slack in unemployment, will extend the fruits of recovery to historically marginalized populations in the labor market and stimulate greater productive investment. Meanwhile, prominent skeptics such as Lawrence Summers, himself a former Treasury secretary, have sounded the alarm about what they see as the significant risks and early signs of inflation, as existing capacity strains to meet the torrent of renewed demand. Implicitly, these admonitions conjure up the specter of the wage-price spirals of the 1970s.

Given the economic landscape since 2008—ultra-low interest rates, reduced worker power, low labor force participation rates—the prospects of this scenario seem rather dim. But the truth is that we don't really know what will happen. The scale of the experiment and the sheer number of moving parts conspire to make forecasts even more uncertain than usual. Every new piece of economic data is scrutinized for auguries, and entire news cycles turn on the finer points of microchip and lumber supply chains or used car sales.

Although uncertainty presents a persistent headache for central bankers and investors, it has a longstanding place in economic theory. Frank Knight, progenitor of the Chicago School of economics in the 1920s, famously distinguished between risk and uncertainty. While *risk* could and should be priced in to routine economic activity, Knight thought, only the heroic entrepreneur could steer his business through the shoals of *uncertainty* in economic life. Profits—otherwise hard to explain within neoclassical theory—were the entrepreneur's reward. Two decades later, Knight's friend Friedrich Hayek made a similar argument from the other end of the stick: given the deep imponderables and complexities of economic affairs, the government had better stick to the sidelines. The unifying message was that economic experimentation should be left to private actors, who alone could assume the personal responsibility of uncertainty.

John Maynard Keynes, by contrast, suggested that it was precisely this inescapable uncertainty that led market participants to favor liquid assets, tilting economies against what neoclassical theory held was a "natural" tendency toward full employment. Correcting the distortion, Keynes thought, required state-led management of aggregate demand, not least for the stability and predictability it would provide. Even in Keynes's case, though, uncertainty was a disquieting reality to be soberly accommodated rather than embraced.

There is one economist from the last century who would have felt rather at home in our moment of uncertainty, however. If any life's work could be summed up by the mantra "We don't know, but let's give it a try," it was that of Albert O. Hirschman, one of the most prominent and original social scientists of the second half of the twentieth century. The subject of a new biography by Italian historian Michele Alacevich, Hirschman theorized a uniquely pragmatic approach to economic management that took surprises for granted—quite unlike the macroeconomics of today. In an era when "crisis" rather than "equilibrium" seems the more obvious tendency of the system, the fascinating experiments of both his life and work may yet have something to teach us.

A COSMOPOLITAN German-born Jewish refugee to France, Britain, Italy, and eventually the United States, Hirschman became a specialist in Latin America and found a wide international audience for his work. Although an economist by training and pioneer of the nascent field of development economics in the 1950s, from practically the outset of his career he pushed against disciplinary boundaries, bringing in tools and concepts from political science, anthropology, the history of ideas, and above all from chance encounters in the field. A onetime Republican volunteer in the Spanish Civil War, undercover fixer in Marseilles for refugees escaping the Nazis, and interpreter at the first Allied war crimes trial, Hirschman completed his peripatetic career by becoming a founding member of the School of Social Science at the prestigious Institute for Advanced Study in Princeton, where he remained until his death in 2012 at the age of ninety-seven. For all this, his intellectual legacy presents something of a paradox: he is, in a sense, both everywhere and nowhere.

On the one hand, Hirschman has few disciples today, and almost none at all in his own field of economics. Some of this might be attributed to the zigzag nature of his scholarly trajectory, and even, as he knowingly put it himself, to his "propensity for self-subversion." But much of it comes down to the incompatibility between his style of thinking and the formal methods that took hold in postwar economics, which increasingly made his ideas marginal or even incomprehensible to initiates of the discipline. In 1995 economist Paul Krugman looked back at the crossroads of the 1950s, in which Hirschman rejected the adoption of strict modeling in development economics which had become practically mandatory everywhere else in the discipline. As he forlornly remarked: "Hirschman didn't wait for intellectual exile: he proudly gathered up his followers and led them into the wilderness himself. Unfortunately, they perished there."

On the other hand, despite this lack of standard-bearers, Hirschman bequeathed a set of concepts, especially in books such as the classic *Exit, Voice, and Loyalty* (1970), that now amount to something like common sense within much of modern social science.

He was a self-consciously public intellectual in his later years, and the remarkable details of his life and his voracious range of interests have kept his ideas in the public eye, as evidenced not least in the wide reception given to Jeremy Adelman's lively biography, *Worldly Philosopher: The Odyssey of Albert O. Hirschman* (2013).

An asset in his role as public intellectual, if possibly a regrettable one for the reception of his work as a whole, was Hirschman's persistent, aphoristic habit of elevating deceptively simple, counterintuitive observations as grand principles of the human condition. The most famous of these, the "Principle of the Hiding Hand" (a knowing nod to Adam Smith's invisible hand), states that in large human undertakings—dam construction, say—we tend to underestimate the difficulties involved. This makes us likelier to get going than we otherwise would have been, had we known all the problems in advance. We also underestimate our creativity in solving problems as they arise, which makes us likelier to succeed than a sober assessment might have determined at the outset:

> The secret of creativity is then to place yourself in situations where you've got to be creative, but this is done only when one doesn't know in advance that one will have to be creative. This, in turn, is so because we underestimate our creative resources; quite properly, we cannot believe in our creativity until we experience it; and since we thus necessarily underestimate our creative resources we do not consciously engage upon tasks which we know require such resources; hence the only way in which we can bring our creative resources into play is by similarly underestimating the difficulty of a task.

Torracinta

Distilled from Hirschman's discussion of major World Bank projects in *Development Projects Observed* (1967), the Hiding Hand was a stimulating provocation, yet on its own it can become little more than a truism. Plucked from their original context, these "Hirschmanisms" have floated freely through the intellectual atmosphere, all too often landing in the pages of national magazines and bestselling airport books. (It is no accident that two of the most prominent and enthusiastic reviewers of Adelman's biography were Malcolm Gladwell and Cass Sunstein.) Further watered down and redigested, they become the kind of chestnuts masquerading as insight duly repeated by the dinner party bore.

Alacevich's new book departs from this fluff Hirschmania to present a compelling, holistic portrait of his scholarly life. His chosen genre of intellectual biography, announced in the book's subtitle, is particularly appropriate for his subject, who treated his career as something like a grand detective novel, letting clues and instincts take him where they may. Essays and even entire books sprouted up from scattered observations in previous research, and conversations with informants on the ground produced additional sets of questions and new, but always provisional, theories. Doubts and unexpected discoveries—all the more delightful because not anticipated—produced loops back to earlier assumptions that fueled his trademark and immensely fertile, if sometimes maddening, self-subversion.

Unlike Adelman's lengthy and colorful page-turner, Alacevich breezes past the many extraordinary episodes of Hirschman's early life in order to focus squarely on his writing. Indeed the book was originally conceived as a primer to the extensive Hirschmanian oeuvre.

What it loses in flair it makes up in comprehensiveness and utility: covering each chapter of his intellectual trajectory in a relatively trim 266 pages, the book serves as an excellent introduction and exegesis, yet also situates each episode of Hirschman's career within a broader, life-long stream of investigation. The drawback of this approach, however, is to lose focus on the wider context in which Hirschman worked: aside from a few mentors, fellow economists, and reviewers of his books, the ideas of others are largely pushed to the margins. Given his fairly astonishing biography, however, readers will likely forgive the attention devoted to the man himself.

BORN IN 1915 to a bourgeois family of assimilated Jews in Berlin, Otto Albert Hirschman was steeped in German *Bildung* from an early age, although one increasingly overshadowed by the steadily building atmosphere of insecurity enveloping German Jews in the interwar years. Presented with a copy of Karl Marx's *Capital* at the age of fourteen by his teacher in the summer of 1930, the young Otto Albert and his sister Ursula were already involved in the Social Democratic Party's radical youth wing as teenagers. It would be a speech that winter at the Berlin Sportspalast by Austrian socialist leader Otto Bauer on no less a weighty subject than Kondratiev long cycles—the idea that the world economy was shaped by half-century long cycles of technological development—that first captivated Hirschman's interest in economics.

The situation in Berlin had so deteriorated by 1933 that, after his father's death in the spring, he set off to study in Paris. In the years to come, the rest of his family inexorably scattered across the continent. For Hirschman, however, this was only the beginning of an Odyssean set of travels throughout the 1930s and 1940s. After a year at the École des Études Commerciales in Paris he moved to the London School of Economics in 1935–36—just in time to catch the explosive reception of John Maynard Keynes's *General Theory* (1936). Only there, Hirschman later recalled, did he "really discover what economics actually is." Alacevich adds that Hayek's LSE lectures on the limits of knowledge in economic processes "struck a chord."

Following a period in the Spanish international brigades in the summer of 1936, fighting in Asturias and Catalonia (a psychologically scarring experience), he traveled to Trieste to rejoin Ursula and her now husband, Italian liberal philosopher Eugenio Colorni, who became a close friend and mentor. It was at the University of Trieste that Hirschman graduated with a thesis in 1938 on recent French monetary policy—an appropriate beginning for a research career in which the political and the economic were always inextricably intertwined. Hirschman secretly joined the antifascist resistance in Italy, smuggling documents across the French border in a false-topped valise. But following the arrest of Colorni (who was later killed by the Nazis in May 1944), and tailed by the Italian political police, Hirschman escaped once again to Paris, finding a position as an economic analyst. With the outbreak of World War II in September 1939, Hirschman enlisted with an émigré company of the French army, but the success of the German Blitzkrieg led to its rapid disbandment.

Slipping south on a stolen bicycle to unoccupied France, Hirschman was recruited in the summer of 1940 by Varian Fry, an American journalist in Marseilles, as an undercover representative of the Emergency Rescue Committee (ERC). Defying both the Vichy and often the American authorities, the ERC sought to smuggle anti-Nazi and Jewish refugees out of southern France to Portugal and onto ferries bound across the Atlantic. A polyglot and general *débrouillard* (as he later described himself), the twenty-five-year-old Hirschman, operating under a pseudonym, became Fry's right-hand man, procuring visas, buying passports, establishing contacts and escape routes. With the gendarmerie asking after him (again) in the winter of 1940, he crossed the Pyrenees himself in December—forgoing most of his belongings except "an extra pair of socks and his copy of Montaigne's *Essais*," writes Adelman—and successfully reached the Lisbon ferry for New York. Over roughly a year, the ERC successfully spirited away Hannah Arendt, Jean Arp, André Breton, Marc Chagall, Marcel Duchamp, Max Ernst, Arthur Koestler, Max Ophüls, Franz Werfel, and thousands of others.

Hirschman's expertise in European economic policy eventually landed him a job in 1946 at the Western European desk of the Federal Reserve Board in Washington, D.C. This fortuitous placement and his connections across the Atlantic saw him closely involved in the postwar European reconstruction, and the Marshall Plan in particular. It was in this hands-on role that he began to develop a set of coordinates that remained with him throughout his career: a reformist and public-spirited ethos; a skepticism of total planning, but not accompanied by any commitment to laissez-faire; and a celebration of creative pragmatism in economic policy.

Torracinta

"A PRIORI DEDUCTIONS," Hirschman wrote in an assessment of Italian reconstruction in 1947, "while instructive, can only yield extremely rough guesses and are not able to replace as yet the method of trial and error." He added, in a sentence that could just as well have been written by heterodox analysts of post-pandemic recovery, that looking for the "correct" aggregate volume of investments in reconstruction was a "futile search." Instead, "one should concentrate upon locating those investments which permit the breaking of important bottlenecks and will thereby lead to increases of output and improvements of performances out of proportion to the investment itself."

For all of Hirschman's radical political engagements and his lifelong anti-fascism, his intellectual and political outlook was far more idiosyncratic than this record might suggest. Whether it was the direct experience of violent dogma, or something deeper in his temperament (or both), he tended to reject capital-letter *-isms* of all kinds. Ultimately he became suspicious of bold, structural theorizing altogether, despite the early influence of Marxism in Berlin. "If Marxism was huge, solid, and imposing intellectual edifice," Alacevich argues, "Hirschman developed instead a predilection for *petites idées*," or little ideas. Or in the favored, playfully oxymoronic phrase of Colorni, "*castelluzzi*"—little castles. Other, less generous assessments are possible, of course. "The fifties effectively smothered him," writes essayist George Scialabba, "as they did all but a very few academic social scientists." Still, Hirschman's broadly social-democratic outlook, pragmatic reformism, and lack of any interest in anti-communism put him at some distance from the emerging Cold War liberal consensus. As he had done in the Pyrenees, here as in many other respects he found himself blazing a trail alone.

Hirschman's trademark intellectual style became evident within his work in development economics, a field he entered practically by accident after preemptively leaving his Fed position to become a financial advisor to the National Planning Council of Colombia in 1952, in the justified fear that his anti-fascist past would expose him to anti-communist repression at the height of McCarthyism. It would be *The Strategy of Economic Development* (1958), written after receiving an appointment at Yale in 1956 and based on reflections on his time in Colombia, that made his reputation.

The contours of development economics had emerged in the late 1940s, as economists sought to apply the lessons of postwar European reconstruction to the broader question of growth and development in the "backward" areas of what was becoming known as the Third World. Dealing with complex, messy realities, with stubborn political and sociological factors, and primarily with long-run growth as opposed to static equilibrium, the field lent itself to unconventional methods quite at odds with the formal models already becoming standard elsewhere in economics—and it led to conclusions about the role of state investment and coordination that broke sharply with received laissez-faire opinion in the profession. It was, in other words, a perfect domain for Hirschman.

By the 1950s, a rough consensus had emerged among pioneering figures such as Paul Rosenstein-Rodan, Ragnar Nurske, and W. Arthur Lewis, in what Krugman has called the period of "high development theory." The general view held that breaking out of the "trap" of low growth under conditions of economic "dualism"—in which the low-wage "traditional" sector failed to generate sufficient demand for a modern, industrial sector—required a central plan of major investments, precisely synchronized to establish a tight network of industries that could sustain a market for each other. A coordinated "Big Push" was therefore necessary to kickstart a self-sustaining, virtuous cycle of investment, but it required a careful approach of "balanced growth" to avoid the risks of particular sectors outgrowing the basis of demand elsewhere in the economy.

Although operating within the same basic framework, Hirschman's *The Strategy of Economic Development* was distinctive in several ways. First, and perhaps most influentially, it insisted on what we might call a "bottom-up" approach to the problem, as opposed to the lofty mountaintop view of the comprehensive plan. In Hirschman's telling, close, on-the-ground observation of successful agricultural or industrial ventures—of "the dynamics of the development process *in the small*"—would yield more insight than "theories dealing with aggregates only or through statistical manipulation involving the division of every conceivable economic variable by the National Income." This approach distilled Hirschman's experience with project investment in Colombia and his suspicions of the rhetoric of planning he heard repeatedly from World Bank economists on the ground—rhetoric he felt was little more than a smokescreen. "The pretense of total, integrated economic planning," he had observed earlier in 1945, "could and often does coexist quite amicably with, and may serve to cover up, unregenerated total improvisation in the actual undertaking and carrying out of investment projects." The point now was not to give up on public coordination but rather to embrace the improvisation.

The Strategy of Economic Development coined the concept of forward and backward "linkages" to focus attention on the upstream and downstream consequences, both expected and unexpected, of development projects. If you invest in a shoe factory, for example, what activity is generated by the heightened demand for leather and by reduced prices for shoes, and what do workers with fatter wage packets choose to spend it on? Simple enough as it may sound to modern ears, this kind of empirical work was not at all common within the grand development theories of the time. In contrast to the "new orthodoxy," Hirschman advocated what he cheekily called "*unbalanced* growth." Planners, he argued, should focus investments on sectors with strong linkages, observe the disequilibrium generated as a consequence, direct the next round of investment to the sector that now needed a push—and then rinse and repeat. One shouldn't plot the entire course of development in advance so much as surf the wave.

Likely the most provocative statement in *The Strategy of Economic Development* was that developing areas were characterized by "one basic scarcity": not scarcity of factors of production like capital (a common refrain in development theory), but scarcity in the ability to make development decisions themselves. Given institutional and economic constraints, the main problem was getting the ball rolling at all. (This was not intended as a cultural comment on "backwardness": indeed, any close observer of infrastructure projects anywhere today will report similar frustrations.) Backward and forward linkages, Alacevich points out, were about preserving scarce decision-making resources: sequential rather than synchronous investment decisions distributed those resources over time. One decision required another in turn, leaving space for contingency and adjustment. Or as Hirschman succinctly put it, "development is essentially the record of how one thing leads to another, and the linkages are that record."

This attention to decisions themselves as both a scarce resource and a catalytic force was the clearest statement of Hirschman's distinctively optimistic and pragmatic brand of reformism. It resonated with what he later called his "possibilism"—his interest, as Alacevich puts it, in "the possible mechanisms through which the process of change could advance—sometimes through inverted, nonlinear, and otherwise unorthodox sequences." As the title of a latter collection of his essays put it, Hirschman indisputably had, for better and for worse, a "bias for hope."

Within a few years of the publication of *The Strategy of Economic Development,* talk of linkages became standard in the field. Indeed the backward linkage approach was fundamental to the import substitution industrialization (ISI) strategies pursued by many Latin American countries through the 1950s and 1960s. Landing a professorship at Columbia in 1958 on the strength of *The Strategy of Economic Development,* Hirschman embarked on a series of works building on its approach. Based on the study of policy problems in Chile, Colombia, and Brazil, his next work, *Journeys Towards Progress* (1963), sought to deconstruct mechanisms of decision-making in a Latin American context, in which change often happened through "highly disorderly sequence."

Against prevailing functionalist theories of modernization that stressed the disharmonious role of social conflict in periods of industrialization, Hirschman charged, for instance, that in societies characterized by lack of effective communication between people and government, mass disruptive protest actually served a useful function of directing attention to neglected problems. He further concluded that failed episodes of reform weren't cause for permanent resignation. Utopian principles that became dead letters, such as those in many Latin American constitutions, could be and often were revived as the basis for new demands decades later. Hirschman slyly likened the book to a "reformmonger's manual," a guidebook to staunch reformists seeking to hack a path through the thicket, offering "some competition to the many handbooks on the techniques of revolutions, coups d'état, and guerilla warfare."

Hirschman's follow up, *Development Projects Observed* (1967), was based on research he and his wife Sarah conducted in assessing thirteen World Bank projects in Latin America, Asia, and Africa. Although overshadowed by the attention accorded to his Principle of the Hiding Hand, the book embodied Hirschman's earlier injunction to understand the dynamics of development "*in the small*." Focusing on three types of development projects—highways, hydroelectric plants, and industries—to understand the distributional and political effects of lending, it was filled with surprising findings. Highway projects, for instance, enhanced the possibility of smallholder, trucking-based entrepreneurship, yet this "means political power, which in turn means the ability to change the rules of the transportation game decisively in favor of the highways." Future decisions to develop other modes of transportation might thus become impossible. A highway also opened up new lands for agricultural exploitation, pushing questions of land ownership higher up the agenda, and could even heighten the risks of ethnic tensions. Yet other types of projects similarly came with their own unique benefits and drawbacks, which could not be captured in the rigid process and arbitrary assumptions of traditional cost-benefit analysis.

Unsurprisingly, the World Bank, which had commissioned the study, was not pleased with these arguments. Hirschman had strayed quite far from economics in any conventional understanding, opening up something like a constructivist theory of social action. "Upon inspection, each project turns out to represent a *unique constellation* of experiences and consequences, of direct and indirect effects," he wrote. "This uniqueness in turn results from the varied interplay between the structural characteristics of projects, on the one hand, and the social and political environment, on the other." One can almost picture the desk officer in D.C. reading the manuscript tearing his hair out.

Development Projects Observed indeed marked a parting of ways, in which development economics was becoming something like an applied field of the mainstream discipline—with all the formal, quantitative methods this implied—while Hirschman became an increasingly uncategorizable social theorist. Despite his statistical and mathematical acuity, Hirschman refused to turn his insights into testable models. Krugman, a fair representative of mainstream disciplinary opinion today, writes that development economics was rescued by adopting "exactly the intellectual attitude Hirschman rejected: a willingness to do violence to the richness and complexity of the real world" by constructing "controlled," simplified models that nevertheless "illustrate key concepts." From this vantage, Hirschman is "not villain in this story so much as a tragic hero."

The idiosyncratic thrust of Hirschman's project was most strikingly illustrated in the famous Hiding Hand, with its practically Deweyan faith in the creative powers of human action—in doing as a kind of thinking. But by the time *Development Projects Observed* was published in 1967, it struck a dissonant note. Confidence in rapid development had begun to ebb worldwide, and many of the Latin American countries dear to Hirschman's heart gave way, one by one, to authoritarian dictatorships. Dramatic social mobilization transformed the political landscape in both the Global North and South. Indeed, there was something about Hirschman's small-scale vignettes and mild-mannered reformism that appeared to countenance an accommodation with the status quo, no matter how untenable or unjust. As he wrote elsewhere the same year:

> Underdevelopment having been diagnosed as something so multifaceted, tangled, and deep-rooted, it was often concluded that the situation called for revolution, massive redistribution of wealth and power from the rich to the poor countries, or at least coordinated attack on pervasive backwardness through highly competent central planning.

> But what if none of these *dei ex machina* are available to take matters properly in hand? What if the fortress of underdevelopment, just because it is so formidable, can not be conquered by frontal assault? In that unfortunately quite common case, we need to know much more about ways in which the fortress can be surrounded, weakened by infiltration or subversion, and eventually taken by similar indirect tactics and processes.

That Third World revolutionaries might reject this counsel for patience is understandable enough. Hirschman's pragmatics of hope could shade into the pragmatics of defeat, and winsome optimism could conceal disillusionment under the surface. Just when Hirschman insisted on thinking small, reformers in the Global South sought to think big, turning to large-scale structural accounts—*dependencia,* world-systems theory—and attempts at global solutions like the New International Economic Order. Within the new turbulent context of the late 1960s and 1970s, Hirschman became an increasingly isolated figure, and his work became more searching and reflective as a result.

THE LANDMARK *Exit, Voice, and Loyalty* (1970) crystallizes this trajectory. Although inspired by observations made during the research for his previous books, the book abstracted away from his field notebooks to produce a model at a new level of generality.

In schematic outline, the book's famous argument runs as follows. In cases of deteriorating service—potholes in a road, say—users are presented with only three options. They can choose *loyalty* by simply sticking it out. They can choose *exit,* for instance by choosing another road or mode of transportation. Or they can choose *voice,* by demanding road repair, say. The abstract concept of voice not only introduced a level of complexity not typically captured by standard microeconomic accounts of behavior, which tended instead to model a binary of loyalty or exit, buying or not buying. It also invited wide application: to "the two-party system, divorce and the American character, black power and the failure of 'unhappy' top officials to resign over Vietnam," as Hirschman put it. In dealing with an adulterous partner, for example, you can put up and shut up, talk it out, or simply leave.

The book was an instant classic. It was reviewed in journals across all of the social sciences and has spawned a still burgeoning secondary literature, a cottage industry of academic work all of its own. This promiscuity owed in part to the book's plasticity: it offered a conceptual vocabulary that could easily—perhaps too easily—be marshalled to make sense of practically any social dynamic. (To be fair, Hirschman was careful to delineate various subtle gradations of "voice" and even "exit" in the book, but these nuances were not what traveled.) As if to signal the culmination of this progressive abstraction, Hirschman was appointed to the rarefied IAS in 1974.

Reflective distance is also one way to read *The Passions and the Interests* (1977), Hirschman's masterpiece of erudition. A brilliant and immensely compelling foray into the history of ideas, Hirschman explicitly acknowledges the book's origin "in the incapacity of contemporary social science to shed light on the political consequences of economic growth and, perhaps even more, in the so frequently calamitous political correlates of economic growth whether such growth takes place under capitalist, socialist, or mixed auspices." Why, Hirschman implicitly asked, had modern social science assumed a direct causal connection between economic and political development? Set against the backdrop of the deepening crises of the 1970s, the book returned to a set of early modern debates—long preceding the disciplinary division between the political and the economic—to discover, as the book's subtitle put it, *Political Arguments for Capitalism before its Triumph.*

In this lively essay of just 135 pages, Hirschman uncovered a rich debate among moral philosophers in the seventeenth and eighteenth centuries in response to the problem of human nature posed forcefully in the Renaissance. Newly unsentimental consideration of man-as-he-is—rather than moralizing homilies of man-as-he-should-be—led to doubts about the unruly and violent "passions" that governed behavior. If, as David Hume succinctly put it, reason was merely the "slave of the passions," by what mechanisms could men be steered toward virtuous, public-minded conduct? By the eighteenth century, Hirschman argued, philosophers began to emphasize the role of countervailing passions—an idea at work, for instance, in the notion of checks and balances in the constitutional debate of the United States. These thinkers fastened on "interest," the cool and rational pursuit of self-benefit, as the best hope for a countervailing force against wilder and more destructive impulses. In the mature, Enlightenment version of this argument, most explicitly articulated by figures such as Montesquieu and James Steuart, the advance of commercial society, in which peace was a more stable environment for doing business, would guarantee the predominance of interest over passion. Hence the idea of *doux commerce*: more than merely economic arrangements, markets would themselves act as civilizing forces.

In its charm and lucidity, the book remains as stimulating as it was when first published. Yet, Alacevich notes, "one might wonder whether this retreat into the history of ideas was not also an act of denial"—leaving behind the failures of development in the present to discover hopes deep in the past. Alacevich adds that reviewers, dazzled by the thesis Hirschman had uncovered, missed the irony pervading the text. The whole starting point of his inquiry had been that such ideas turned out to be totally wrong. At the same time, the reviewers could perhaps be cut a little slack. For despite a few cryptic remarks in the final section, Hirschman mostly refuses to reflect on the implications of these failed predictions, much less spell out an alternative theory. The end of the book simply remarks that "speculations about the salutary political consequences of economic expansion were a feat of imagination in the realm of political economy, a feat that remains magnificent even though history may have proven [them] wrong." This leads to the rather deflating conclusion that "all one can ask of history, and of the history of ideas in particular" is "not to resolve issues, but to raise the level of debate." A new level of reflective distance, indeed.

Had the book been written a few years later, Hirschman might have taken a different tack. Prophets of the age of Reagan such as Milton Friedman had no qualms about trotting out a substance-free version of the *doux commerce* thesis as and when it suited them. (If this was tragedy, the bargain-basement approximations of this argument associated with the likes of Thomas Friedman are surely farce.) Disturbed by the rise of the New Right and its intransigence in the face of state intervention, Hirschman, still a social democrat at heart, responded belatedly to this moment with *The Rhetoric of Reaction* (1991).

Torracinta

Tracing the rise of reactionary ideas following the French Revolution, in a rather eclectic mix of thinkers from Edmund Burke to Charles Murray, Hirschman sought to delineate three basic responses to any proposed reform: the perversity thesis (it will achieve the opposite of its intent); the futility thesis (it won't work at all); and the jeopardy thesis (it will put other accomplishments at risk). But in a moment of characteristically acrobatic self-subversion, Hirschman then turned this analysis right around onto progressive proponents of reform to detail three mirror theses of apparently equal intransigence: the counter-perversity thesis (this reform is needed or we face total ruin); the counter-futility thesis (the laws of history demand the reform, so opposition is futile); and the counter-jeopardy thesis (only this new reform can save older achievements). Each of these moves is still recognizable in the present. Understanding these structures of argument, Hirschman suggested, might clear the ground for mutual disarmament of the rhetorical arsenal. Yet while an interesting exercise, the symmetry may look to many readers today like an inert plea for dialogue and compromise couched in criticism of "both sides."

WHAT ARE WE TO MAKE of this complex legacy? There remain a few Hirschmanian figures still scattered across the academy (the probing economist Dani Rodrik comes to mind). But in retrospect, ambitious balanced and unbalanced growth programs had more in common with each other than with the ideas that succeeded them: consider the socially devastating "reforms" imposed on developing countries by the IMF's structural adjustment programs in the 1980s. Ironically, given the abeyance into which they fell in that period, many foundational insights of high development theory have been reincorporated since then—in appropriate mathematical form—into the models of development economics of recent decades. The great inflation debate of 2021 makes it clear, however, that no matter how sophisticated or powerful they may be, models remain a highly contested feature of contemporary economics. Given the theoretical rigidity, mathematical formalism, and fierce professional hierarchy of the mainstream discipline today, Hirschman's early skepticism of these trends looks more prescient than tragic.

Perhaps the more interesting question is whether we find ourselves in what economist Ilene Grabel has called a "Hirschmanian moment." She coined the term to describe the "productive incoherence" of post-2008 global financial governance, in which "many emerging markets and developing economies have escaped the straitjacket of a commanding theoretical orthodoxy" and the "prescribed menu of institutional forms." But the metaphor could be further extended to our broader political economic conjuncture. Within the rusty carapace of the neoliberal order, old rules increasingly appear to no longer apply. At the same time, what comes next is exceptionally difficult to predict. But incoherence, as Hirschman counseled, is also an opportunity.

To many, Hirschman's ebullient miniatures will appear dated and inadequate in the face of concatenating crises—economic, ecological, epidemiological, political—that cry out for ambitious structural explanation and major social transformation. And yet something in Hirschman's pragmatism may be worth holding on to in coming to terms with what they require. We lack detailed, tried-and-tested blueprints for the truly massive scale of social, economic, and technological change required for transition to a zero-carbon economy, for instance—or for a post-capitalist transition of any kind. If Hirschman is to be believed, however, we could never fully know these things in advance: the only way to figure them out would be to try. If the system does turn out to be too corrupt, exhausted, or inert to offer up any meaningful change, it may be that "exit" of some kind really is the only option. But what if that isn't on the table, at least not in the foreseeable future? (Do we have any escape routes across the mountains left?) To storm what Russian revolutionary Alexandra Kollontai once called the "beleaguered fortress of the future," perhaps indirect Hirschmanian measures will be required.

Radicals and reformers alike may need to embrace the uncertainty of the present, to make a virtue of improvisation, to seek out the exasperatingly disordered, nonlinear, incoherent, and unexpected sequences by which the status quo is always and ever undermined. In the "creative disorder of the human adventure," Hirschman wrote in *A Bias for Hope* (1971), "radical reformers are unlikely to generate the extraordinary social energy they need to achieve change unless they are exhilaratingly conscious of writing an entirely new page of human history." One of the basic affects of our bewildering present is systematic and pervasive doubt. As far as Hirschman was concerned, so much the better.